Milk and Whiskey

On Logan Way

a memoir

Timothy Burke, LICSW

ISBN: 979-8-8640-8339-0

Book design:
Y42K Publishing Services
https://www.y42k.com/publishing-services/

One day, you will tell the story of how you overcame what you went through, and it will be someone else's survival guide.

—Anonymous

Note from the author:

I'm grateful for the fellowship of recovering alcoholics who have preceded me in my journey toward sobriety. They are living examples of men and women of dignity and honor who, by their commitment to recovery, continue to inspire and offer hope to those struggling with alcoholism. Their unwavering support, empathy, and guidance have been instrumental in my personal growth and recovery. They have been there for me and many others every step of the way.

I have five brothers I love deeply, all of whom were raised by our parents in the same household. However, out of respect for their privacy, I have focused solely on my journey. Each one has his reality and has responded to life's challenges in his own way. I'm grateful that each of them has been a source of support and encouragement for me on my journey. Their support has made the burden of my struggles much lighter.

CONTENTS

Prologue

Since my first year of college, I had a burning desire to write about my early beginnings. Even then, I was keenly aware of the challenging and confusing circumstances of my journey. At that time, I had no idea what the ending of my story would be, yet I was determined to write about it. I would have been surprised by the complex and dangerous path I took and how it shaped me into the person I am today. Indeed, I could not have imagined that my life would unfold as it did because I would never have chosen the path I took.

This tale is my own Odyssey, in which my resilience, versatility, and cleverness nearly led me to jail or an early grave. I consider myself fortunate to be alive today. This is a story of suffering, recovery, and redemption. My teenage years into my early thirties were the height of my alcohol and drug abuse, a period in my life when I could not be creative, productive, or at peace with myself. It was a time when I made futile attempts to control people with my all-or-not thinking and perfectionism to ease my pain and avoid shame. I was a square peg in a round hole, driven by fear, rage, and resentment, uncomfortable in my own skin. I never wanted you to know it because you wouldn't understand or be able to offer me the help I so desperately needed.

This memoir has been simmering for forty-plus years and repeatedly delayed because I was not fully liberated from alcoholism, trauma, and abuse. My struggle has been volatile, a pleading to escape the confines of trauma and shame. The past thirty-two years of my life have not been without challenges.

9

Because I found recovery, these years have been the best years of my life. This is the direct result of the men, women, and suggestions of a twelve-step recovery program I reluctantly was introduced to. Today, I can say that I am grateful for my life, which has been surprisingly satisfying after a difficult beginning.

That does not mean I've been able to escape my past completely. Painful memories can still surface in my mind without reason or warning. When this happens, I replay the tapes of my past in search of a different outcome. *If only I had been born in another time or place, if only I had another family, if only...* The memories are distant, but the sentiment is the same, a regretful *"if only"* tinged with anger and sadness. Despite years of recovery, I sometimes feel resentment and irritability over my past—painful feelings born from the intrusions of an eternal yesterday. It is as if I have an emotional hangover from my past. A day had not gone by when I didn't think I'd had enough that now was the time to move on and have the life I was supposed to have. My life has been a journey of ups and downs, with successes, disappointments, and heartache. It would have been much better had I let go of the past demons long ago. Today, I strive for acceptance, gratitude, and forgiveness. Forgiveness leads to freedom, enabling me to be my true self.

I needed the emotional pain to subside and to be reconciled to it so that I could understand and articulate my experiences and talk about my life with others. I am an average Joe, neither a rock star nor a celebrity. I'm just another Bozo on the bus. This journey took many years until I figured out a graceful and humble way to cross the finish line of life.

I am writing this memoir for several compelling reasons. First, to offer hope and support to other survivors of trauma and abuse. In today's world, countless families are grappling with the same experiences I endured as a child. While many have faced even more severe and tragic events than I have, within the depths of any traumatic experience, it feels like the worst thing that could happen to you. Trauma can be overwhelmingly isolating. Perhaps my story can be a guiding light for anyone, whether it's a child, a spouse, or someone you know trapped in the dysfunction of another person's addiction to extricate themselves from this insidious disease. Maybe my account will offer solace to teenagers living in unhealthy, toxic, and traumatic environments. I want to emphasize that victimhood does not have to define us. There was hope for me, and there is hope for you. Just as there is help for those struggling with addiction, there is also help for those harmed by an alcoholic. Resources are available, and you are not alone on this journey. With assistance and knowledge, we can discover the strength, wisdom, and beauty within ourselves.

Second, I would like to show that every person has unique experiences in life, and these experiences should be considered without judgment. Just like all of us, the homeless or jobless person on the streets has a story and is on a journey. Their stories are often complicated, sad, and harrowing. For some, the outcomes are mostly unfavorable, and they may feel trapped in trauma with no escape, trying desperately to make it through another day without a drink. Surviving or thriving is a dilemma familiar to many who experience addiction and trauma. When I gaze into the eyes of a homeless person, I now see much more than some "wino" begging for change to buy a bottle of cheap alcohol. I realize that I could easily be looking at myself. People need to recognize that much more is happening within those they might dismiss as mere "drunks and junkies." In our world, we must slow down, listen, and learn more about each other. To better understand, we need to practice compassion instead of condemnation, as we never know who may be silently crying themselves to sleep at night.

Finally, in sharing my story of hope and recovery, I aim to offer valuable insight to those entangled by addiction and to those non-alcoholics who may not fully grasp the emotional turbulence that often characterizes the tragic life of an alcoholic. For those battling alcoholism or mental health issues, life can sometimes feel devoid of spirituality, leading to a profound sense of separation from God and agonizing loneliness. Alcoholics frequently experience feelings of abandonment, being misunderstood, and a profound sense of brokenness. The emotional abyss and isolation in which active alcoholics find themselves can be difficult for non-alcoholics to comprehend fully.

For many, the pain caused by an alcoholic to their loved ones may never completely heal, as these wounds are both painful and profound. This is the harsh reality of alcoholism. But remember this straightforward truth: you are not alone, and there is hope and healing.

PART 1

Growing Up in The Project

Children have never been very good at listening to
their elders, but they have never failed to imitate
them.
-James Baldwin

I was born and raised in "Southie," the predominantly Irish, working-class neighborhood within the City of Boston, officially known as South Boston. This densely populated area is located east of the Fort Point Channel and abuts Dorchester Bay. This area was annexed to the city of Boston in 1804. Our neighborhood made national news in the early 1970s because of the community's strong opposition to federally mandated forced busing and court-ordered public school integration. This mandate compelled low-income children from South Boston to attend schools in low-income Roxbury, a predominantly Black community, rather than schools in the immediate neighborhood. Like the other two public housing projects in South Boston, the housing project I resided in was in the neighborhood's lower-end or less affluent part.

Ours was a tight-knit community where street-smart kids learned to grow up fast and hard, unfazed by circumstances that would send suburban kids running home crying to their mothers. Today, I realize just how desensitized I was to that violence. We were the only neighborhood in Boston with its own theme song—"Southie is My Hometown." After a few beers, this tune was often sung at social events, and we learned it as a rite of passage. The neighborhood's most prominent institutions were the Church, politics, and sports. The many churches in Southie played a central role in religious and social activities in the community. You could only be "from Southie" if you were born there. If you moved into the community, there was always skepticism, and you would be reminded that you weren't from Southie—you were temporarily living there. God forbid that you move out. Then you were considered an arrogant turncoat who thought he was better than everyone else!

Our community had seven Catholic parishes, one Polish and one Lithuanian church. Each local area took pride in its parish and boasted of its uniqueness. This pride sometimes turned into heated arguments or the occasional fistfights. Even the local priests took pride in their parish.

I vividly recall being reprimanded by the Monsignor in The Gate of Heaven grammar school due to my poor grades. I struggled academically as a kid and had to repeat the second and fifth grades. The Monsignor was there to hand out report cards, distributed according to the highest to lowest grades. All of the bright, shining stars went way ahead of me. The kids before me were two brothers called up to receive their report cards from the Monsignor. He scolded them in front of the class. Suddenly, he swung a backhander across the face of one of them while catching the other on the side of his head. Two fifth graders with one backhander! This guy had fast hands, and I was up next. I thought I was a dead kid walking. (You didn't tell your parents that the teacher yelled at you or hit you because you would get it again at home.) I defiantly approached the Monsignor when my name was called. In front of my fifth-grade class, he expressed his dismay at my report card and ended the verbal shaming by saying, "You're not even from this parish. I'm not even going to bother smacking you!" I didn't flinch. I stared at him, thinking, go ahead and smack me. I just wanted this over. Then I thought about getting back at him if he hit me. Maybe I should torch his car, I thought. After that year, my parents pulled me out of parochial school and placed me in the local public school. So long, Sisters and Brothers!

The "lower end" kids would constantly battle with the kids from City Point, the "lace curtain entitled kids." City Point had better homes, and City Point kids went to parochial or private schools and had a good life. I remember our state senator joking that he could tell which kids were from City Point because they all had beautiful white teeth and wore polished Penny Loafer shoes. While the kids from the lower end were missing teeth and wore sneakers with holes in the soles. Nevertheless, we always came together to battle any outsider who attacked, verbally or physically, anyone from Southie.

The community I grew up in was very patriotic. During the Vietnam War, many young men from Southie enlisted in the service before they were drafted. As a teen, I recall reading stories in our local newspaper about groups of guys who hung out together on a corner and who all joined to serve under a buddy system. South Boston established the first community memorial in the United States for men killed in the Vietnam War. Twenty-five names were inscribed on the memorial, each a soldier from Southie who died in action. This is the largest group of men killed in action from a community this size in the country. My friends and I contemplated joining the Army, but we were too young to be drafted. When the government changed the draft to a lottery system, my number was too high; the war was over by then. Thank

God because I would later witness firsthand the trauma and emotional scars the Vietnam War left on many of these men. Many got caught up in the alcohol and drugs scene and paid a heavy price.

Most outsiders either love or loathe Southie's community spirit. This spirit bonded the neighborhood and created a large voting block that politicians coveted. The Boston press disliked the community and appeared determined to break South Boston's hold on Boston politics, sports, and social issues. But as the lyrics to "Southie Is My Hometown" remind us:

"We have doctors and flappers,
Preachers and scrappers,
Men from the Old County Down.
They will take you and break you,
But they'll never forsake you;
For Southie is my hometown."

I was number four of six boys in my family, and we lived on Logan Way in the Old Harbor Housing Project, which was the first public housing development in New England. When I was growing up in the projects, most men living there had returned from World War II. They needed affordable housing to start their families. Many families had a two-parent home, typical of the times, with Dad working and Mom working part-time, often as a waitress. Dad was a Boston firefighter and worked a second job as a union truck driver for a construction supply company. As a kid in grammar school, I would jump up from my seat and run to the window when a firetruck passed by our school and proclaim, "That's my father's firetruck! He's a firefighter!" I felt special because my Dad rode on that big red truck with the giant ladder, racing through our city to save someone's life and extinguish a fire. Whenever a firetruck roared by with sirens blaring, I watched with pride because that was my Dad, who was invincible.

I was also very proud of my Mom because she worked two jobs as a waitress and a school crossing guard for the City of Boston. She was born on March 7, 1919, and raised in the Roslindale neighborhood on top of a hill with a beautiful view of Boston. She was also from a large family of three boys and three girls. She had a difficult start in life. Her father, an immigrant from Ireland, was a Boston Police patrolman who lost his job due to the 1919 police strike and never worked again in law enforcement or for any public agency. The public civil service offices "blackballed" these men, and many, like my grandfather, had to work sporadic menial jobs. This event impacted Mom's family's finances, but she never complained.

In addition to working part-time, my mother's primary and most appreciated role was to take care of all six boys while being a loving wife. It was reassuring to see Mom dressed in her official school crossing guard uniform, stopping traffic, and guiding the other children across the street when I walked home from school. She knew most of the kids' names and often would chat with them and have something positive to say while inquiring about each kid and their family. Being in that vital role in our community gave Mom access to critical information, neighborhood gossip, and tips on the day-to-day life of the housing project. She always had a smile and a positive attitude. She was never shy about speaking up to right an injustice in the neighborhood. If a kid bullied someone in the schoolyard, Mom would hear about it. She would pull them aside and confidently tell them to *knock it off, or I'll tell your parents.*

After that, she would make friends with the offending students by recalling their names and talking to them about their day in school while directing traffic.

Somehow, while caring for six kids and Dad, Mom managed to have a group of close women friends in the project. Whenever I met someone who knew my Mom, they often said, "What a beautiful lady your Mom is," or "I don't know how she does it." Her friends commented that her beautiful complexion was "so smooth and clear." I knew her secret was to apply inexpensive moisturizer each night as we sat in the living room and watched television. She would use a heavy layer of cold cream on her face and then remove it with tissue from the box on the coffee table. She went through many tissues, and the smell of the cold cream permeated the living room. Today, whenever I smell that inexpensive drug store cold cream, it evokes cherished memories of Mom. It worked well for her because her friends continued commenting on how beautiful Mom's face appeared for many years.

The Old Harbor Project was large, with more than a thousand apartments in three-story buildings and 150-row houses, which we called townhouses because that sounded more attractive. These units were outstanding by public housing standards, and Mom and Dad were fortunate to live in one of them. Despite the constricted conditions, the townhouses were considered special living accommodations. Some friends joked that our family had won the ghetto lottery by "scoring" a townhouse. It included a cramped two-and-a-half bedroom, one bathroom, and a small living room that Mom insisted on calling the "parlor." The small kitchen also served as a dining room. The washer and dryer stood side-by-side a few steps from the stove. There were no vents in the project kitchens. You open the window every season to remove the smoke or steam. A circular wooden plate hung above the electric stove and partially covered the fuse box with the words "God Bless our Home." Because of its location, it was often covered in a splattering of grease. It's the one thing I saved from our house in the project, and today, it hangs in my home.

The floor, a worn linoleum with scratches and holes from the sports equipment my brothers and I lugged across, gave the entire space an institutional feel. The sink resembled a large industrial basin supported by imposing white porcelain legs with an open area below that was used for storage. Above the sink hung a small wooden shelf painted white, on which Mom thumb-tacked two laminated cards: the prayer of St. Patrick and a poem called "Don't Quit." These inexpensive water-stained cards hung there for many years and provided wisdom and solace we could read while washing dishes. I memorized the poem "Don't Quit" and, with determination, would quietly recite it to myself when things were not going well. There were many occasions when things did not go well in our home, and I often contemplated quitting. This poetry was also particularly fitting when it came to pursuing an education: "Rest if you must, but do not quit." I took these words to heart and persevered.

My parents turned a part of the unfinished basement into an additional bedroom by putting up some wood studs, drywall, and wood veneer paneling—the same wood paneling my mother installed in the living room and kitchen (even though this was against the rules in the project). This remodeling turns our project townhouse into a home. The manager of this development, Mr. Mead, once scolded me for digging up dirt with a metal serving spoon and making holes in our meager yard. He looked at me, then knocked on our door, and told my Mom to "Stop him from digging in the yard!" She complied until I was back in the yard playing in the dirt the next day. That was our "sandbox."

The basement bedroom was small, but we barely managed to fit a twin bed into it. Our hockey sticks and other sports equipment hung from the heat, waste, and water lines above us on the ceiling. The iron pipes were covered in asbestos insulation and banged and rattled during the winter. Few were aware of the dangers of asbestos in those days. Sleeping in the basement also meant climbing two sets of stairs to the second floor to use the only bathroom in our townhouse. This was a minor inconvenience for the luxury of "private" space, which was almost sacred to us kids. Naturally, this highly coveted bedroom went to my oldest brother. Each time one of my brothers moved out, the remaining brothers switched beds.

The units in the development had solid cast iron radiators for heat that the Boston Housing Authority generously and continuously supplied from early October to the middle of April. The only way to control the excessive temperature from the radiators was to open a window. We often joked that the snow would blow through one window and out the other. When the windows were open in the summer, we could smell smoke from the apartment building's incinerators. This would never be allowed today, but in my early years, smoke and ashes often floated everywhere, and it would be unfortunate for your family if your mom had the laundry drying outside. You could get covered in soot on the garbage-burning day if you played outside or just hung out with friends. Some kids often ignited the hallway incinerator and watched it burn for fun. The trash chute kept us warm in the winter when we lingered in the hallway, drinking, playing cards, strumming guitars, and singing.

Summertime was equally uncomfortable. July and August were sweltering, and each building held in the brutal, oppressive heat like a brick oven. At times, it felt like I was sleeping in a kiln. I would lie in bed dripping with sweat, trying to sleep in the crowded bedroom where the four of us boys slept in two sets of bunk beds.

The project had hundreds of apartments full of families, and there was always a plentiful supply of kids to play with. Because there were so many kids living in the project, we always had many friends to hang with. We knew which cellars and roof doors were unlocked, and sometimes, we played hide-and-seek in the basements or hallways. The basement cellars and roofs were quite an advantage when we tried to avoid getting caught by enemies, kids outside our project, or the cops. Small gravel stones were always scattered around the roof, and we threw them at unsuspecting outsiders or anyone who ventured into our territory.

The courtyard of our modest brick-and-mortar building was covered with the hottest and blackest asphalt I've ever seen, felt, or smelled. The asphalt yards were always busy with kids playing Red Rover, basketball, stickball, tag, street hockey, or football games. There were very few grass-covered fenced-in grounds to play on. My favorite game was "Kill the Man with the Ball." One of us would grab the football, run through a line of kids, and avoid getting tackled. Most of us never made it through the line, and once attacked, there would always be a "pile on." Amazingly, we survived this pummeling without wearing any protective equipment. The fun part was knocking someone on his ass. We were scrappy kids.

Many sights and smells bring me back to those days and stir up vivid childhood memories. Some are painful, others are happy. Each season had its particular odor in the air. In the spring, bushes, and trees grew all around the housing development. I thought we were special because we had an abundance of perennial spirea bushes with fragrant white blooms throughout the housing development. We also had plenty of maple and crab apple trees, which show their buds in springtime. Many families, including mine, had a small patch of dirt to grow a few tomato plants. Like many families, our heavy galvanized steel trash barrels shared the same space as the tomato plants outside the back door. Fall smelled of delicious food prepared in our house by Mom, especially Sunday dinners that would resume after the summer. I enjoyed Sunday family dinners. Winter was when the hot radiators would warm the dust collected between the pipes, creating a musty odor as soon as the project management turned the heat on.

Despite this rather bleak environment, there were many happy times. On a typical day, we woke up, walked downstairs through the parlor, and entered the kitchen, where my mother would greet each of us with a song: *"Good morning, little yellow bird, yellow bird, yellow bird. Good morning little yellow bird. How are you today?"* She gave each of us a big hug and a kiss, and we always felt loved by her, even during the midst of difficulty in our home.

We were lucky that our family was one of a few who owned a car. It was a Ford station wagon, which we named the "beach wagon" because we spent plenty of days at the beach or a lake. Mom and Dad would load up a large metal cooler filled with a big block of ice, burgers, hotdogs, soda, and beer. It was so heavy that only my father could carry it. We had a small, flimsy charcoal grill that Dad was responsible for lighting with a square can of lighter fluid that only he could touch. Occasionally, he would pour on extra lighter fluid to entertain us kids, and we would be in awe at the leaping flames.

At the start of every family trip, we said a short prayer. Dad would remove his blue bucket hat and lead us in prayer, asking the Lord for a safe journey. A Saint Christopher medal sat beside a Smokey the Bear ashtray on the car's dashboard. My father attended church every week. At home, we always said grace before meals and were instructed to pray before bed. I often thought that he prayed because of the importance and dangers of his job as a firefighter.

Mom took excellent care of us. She occasionally prepared treats like chocolate chip cookies, fresh-baked bread, or a glass of homemade eggnog. Whenever one of us had a cold, we received a cup of tea and some buttered toast sprinkled with cinnamon sugar. My favorites were the oatmeal raisin cookies and Irish bread. There was always a wonderful home-cooked meal on Sundays and holidays. Mom usually improved standard fare with some unique touch, adding something to the stew or the side of vegetables. On holidays, she made the most delicious turkey gravy from scratch. I enjoyed helping her and learning how to cook. I spent time with Mom and discovered her secret recipe for that special turkey gravy. Some fifty years later, I am still asked to make Mom's gravy at family get-togethers. The smell and taste of that gravy take my brothers and me back to the small apartment in the project and give us the feeling that Mom is still with us. Nieces and nephews, family friends, and in-laws all ask what's in it as they pour themselves another hearty spoonful. My reply is always the same: "If I told you, it wouldn't be a secret." (The secret, you ask? Open a twelve-ounce Bottle of Knickerbocker beer, pour half in, add a pinch of salt to the gravy, and drink the other half. Please don't let my brothers know I told you.)

Growing up, each of us kids received one present at Christmas. These were primarily practical gifts like clothing and sometimes much-valued sports equipment. Occasionally, a community toy for all to enjoy appeared under the tree. Our "Christmas stockings" were white athletic socks thumbtacked or nailed to the back of a solid wooden door. The other sock would be rolled up and tucked inside—we needed both socks to wear to our next hockey game—along with an orange, an apple, some walnuts, a candy cane, and some chocolate-covered candy wrapped in golden foil resembling gold coins. Occasionally, we received a roll of multicolored Life Savers—mysteriously, so did every kid in the project. Overall, it wasn't much. It was very modest compared with what many of my project friends had for Christmas, including their fancy red-and-white Christmas stockings with their names written in silver glitter across the top. But we could depend on it, and I knew that my athletic socks were offered with love, and we were grateful to have them. During these early years, Christmas was a happy time.

We would get a birthday cake and a small present each year on our birthdays. My paternal grandmother gave each of us a birthday card with a one-dollar bill. She never forgot us. Never. As a teenager, I sometimes jokingly complained about the insignificance of a dollar. But over the years, I have forgotten all my other birthday presents, while I still remember that dollar bill from my grandmother. She never forgot our birthdays. Even today, sixty-eight years later, my brothers and I give each other a "buck" on birthdays.

I look forward to this gesture and its meaningful reminder that I am loved and remembered. I appreciate sharing that with my brothers.

South Boston Boys Club

The South Boston Boys Club, a branch of the Boys Club of Boston, is less than a mile from the project. This clubhouse was founded in 1938, and today, it's called the Boys and Girls Club of Boston and has ten clubs around the city serving over 14,000 boys and girls. The clubhouse was always filled with kids of all shapes, sizes, and athletic abilities from all over South Boston, especially kids from housing projects. The club members included great athletes, tough street fighters, budding criminals, and nerdy bookworms. Everyone was willing to teach you what they knew, and there was occasionally kindness and encouragement.

For me, the club was a respite from the increasing domestic troubles that I was experiencing at home. Many kids used the Boys Club as a place to find relief from the dysfunction in their homes. The club was where I could go and immerse myself in many different activities, mainly sports, reading books, and shooting pool. By age fifteen, I owned a two-piece pool cue and dreamed of being a hustler in Las Vegas. I was already hustling other kids on the pool table as I had learned to do from the older kids who had cheated me. I learned to play checkers from an old guy named Doc, who gave us three or four candy Sugar Babies when we played against him. I graduated from checkers to chess, started playing in the library, and could hold my own against many older guys.

Like any club, this one had a hierarchy of members, grouped mainly by age. I usually played and hung around with guys my age. Still, I always looked for opportunities to hang with the older guys. Many older guys would use a wet towel whip, known as a "rat tail," to snap and hit another guy in the locker room. *Man, did that hurt!* Often, some unsuspecting kid would come walking out of the showers to be met by some bully with a wet towel snapping it, with speed and accuracy, trying to hit them in the balls! I've seen kids with welts on the back of their asses from getting hit with a "rat tail." Not fun! You got dressed quickly to avoid getting hit. I know of two kids who never returned to the club after experiencing a "rat tail."

Growing up in a house with five brothers, I learned how to stand up for myself against bullies and fight back. In my house, it seemed as though I was always wrestling or punching one or two of my brothers. I've been hit by a "noogie" or knuckle sandwich for no reason many times by one or two of my brothers. I also gave a few good ones that left a bruise or two. The most memorable one happened after I had to get a tetanus shot in my arm. I had stepped on a rusty nail that penetrated deep into my foot. Mom took me to the hospital for a tetanus shot. When I returned, my brother Kevin, sounding compassionate, asked me if the needle hurt. I said it did. "Let me see where it hurts," he said. I roll up my sleeve to show him where the needle had gone into my arm. Bam! He punched me in the exact spot. I screamed as I tried to grab him by the throat and take him down. He ran away laughing, yelling, "I bet it hurts now!" Mom had to break up our many wrestling matches like a hockey referee. Mom would yell at us multiple times for getting too physical in the living room. Our living room parlor was an excellent training ring. I don't know how she put up with us six boys.

At the Boys Club, I also learned some tricks the management frowned on, such as stealing from someone's locker. There never was anything of value in a gym locker because everyone was poor. Maybe we'd take some loose change or an inexpensive Timex watch. The cast of characters at the Boys Club was wide-ranging, and I learned to determine who was a physical threat, who had smarts, and who was a phony. Other skills I learned at the Club included photography and cooking. I enjoyed the cooking classes, and I could step up to prepare dinner for the family if Mom was unavailable or I was in the mood to cook something special.

The cooking instructor was Howie Bunkley. He was outgoing, pleasant, and flamboyant. He always remembered your name and had a wide smile. Howie was well-liked by all the kids at the Club, and for many, including me, he was our first experience interacting with a Black person. It was not a common sight to see a man of color in our predominantly segregated neighborhood. Still, it seemed as though everyone accepted and respected Howie. He was a good man.

My Mom and Dad had the opportunity to meet Howie at one of the dinners our cooking class prepared for our parents. Howie had something positive to say about our cooking or baking skills. We all beamed with pride as he introduced us individually and had us explain what and how we had prepared for the dinner. It was a magical and exciting occasion. My parents and Howie connected when my Dad discovered that Howie lived right around the corner from my Dad's firehouse.

Two weeks later, my father came home to let me know he had seen Howie that day while driving the fire truck in the South End. Howie, being the excited person he was, started jumping up and down at the sight of my Dad driving the Tiller of the firetruck. At the same time, the other firefighters stared in awe, trying to figure out how my Dad knew this bald Black man waving his handkerchief at him. I imagine Dad had much explaining to do when he returned to the firehouse that evening.

Because of my Mom and what I could learn at the Boys Club, I could prepare everyday meals and holiday dinners in our home. When I cooked, my brothers often jokingly complained that the meal was not great, but I noted they always ate it all and frequently wanted more. I also believe that sitting down to dinner with each other helped keep my brothers and me together as a family when we faced challenging times.

Being a member of the Boys Club meant learning social skills and respect for others. It also meant learning to fend for and respect yourself, a valuable life lesson for anyone. When the gym instructor was absent, there were no rules in some of the games we played, like dodgeball or bombardment (a variation of dodgeball), other than not crossing the center court line. Inattention to the game risked injury by a flying red rubber ball. I saw kids get knocked down and cry, only to jump up shouting that they would *kill the mf...* that threw that ball. Some sneaky kids stood on the sidelines as though they weren't in the game, only to pull a ball out from under the back of their shirt and whip it at some kid's face, resulting in a bloody nose. Again, you would hear someone shout, *shut the f-- up and sit down, you faggot!* Some kids would roll a ball toward an opponent, appearing to be doing the guy a favor only to set him up for an attack. Kids who jumped in the air to avoid getting hit often had their legs knocked out from under them for a hard landing on their side or shoulder. Welts, black eyes, bloody noses, and hurt feelings were a standard part of the game. But despite all the casualties, there was never a shortage of kids willing to play. We loved the free-for-all games without rules.

The games were the same in high school but were played with much more skill and force, resulting in visits to the nurse's office. We encouraged one another to be a bit crazy, like gladiators. Kill or be killed was the goal. On more than one occasion, the male teachers visited the gym during their smoke break (yes, they smoked cigarettes in the break room those days) to watch the carnage.

Swimming did not have as many admirers as contact sports, but I was in my element in the pool. Whenever there was a problem at home or in school, as there frequently was, being in the swimming pool was like being in a meditation room. Sometimes, just being a kid can be challenging, but this was a calming refuge, my place to escape. I loved swimming and preferred this over any other activity. My Mom taught me how to swim at Carson Beach. The same beach I was assigned to as a lifeguard years later. I'm unsure how to describe it, but swimming was peaceful and relaxing. The pool was available every day of the week the club was open, and I could purchase a "swim check" and gain entrance to my Nirvana for two cents.

One thing that was maybe peculiar to the South Boston Boys Club was that swimming in the nude was the norm. It indeed broke down any fears about being self-conscious. The only time we didn't swim "bare ass" was during swim meets when all competitors wore a Speedo bathing suit. However, I always thought Speedos were for sissies and that real men swim in the nude. My friends and I swam throughout the year. Locker rooms were not equipped with hairdryers back then, so during the winter, our hair would freeze on the walk home, and we would laugh at each other, trying to break the icicles off our hair.

Friends and Characters

All six Burke boys were actively involved in sports. At the same time, my parents were instrumental in initiating and organizing the youth hockey program in South Boston, which continues to thrive. Their outgoing personalities made them highly popular and respected for their dedication to youth sports programs.

Many meetings throughout the year occurred at our kitchen table and often went late into the evening. Alcohol was always present at these get-togethers, and frequently, the discussion would evolve into a party. The record player—a rather large, well-worn console given to us by our Uncle Tom—stood in the living room and blared Irish music by the end of a meeting. We kids were shuffled off to bed, where we were expected to sleep despite the noise and excitement. The laughing and singing were occasionally very loud, frequently leading to Irish step dancing in our tiny living room. I enjoyed hearing the Irish music and learned many of the songs. Many of these songs were drinking songs, such as The Wild Rover: *"I've been a wild rover for many years. And I spent all me money on whiskey and beer. But now I'm returning with gold in great store. And I never will play the wild rover no more."*

I did not think about the problems at home when I was with friends. I would be willing to bet that many of my friends were hanging out to avoid the dysfunction in their homes—not that hanging out was always a source of positivity, but it could be a soothing respite from the fear and dysfunction at home. We enjoyed each other's company because we shared the same problems and a similar nihilistic outlook on life. Family life was difficult for many, and pessimism was widespread in the project.

But I never laughed more than when hanging out with friends. Much of our banter was gallows humor, laughing and joking at our misfortune or the misfortune of others in our circle of acquaintances. We were all quick-witted and fast on our feet when making up a joke, a comeback, or a sarcastic remark. The sarcasm we learned from the adults in the project. Many adults, not all, would offer a compliment only to follow it with cutting sarcasm. I did feel the protection that was a part of growing up in the project. We looked out for one another and always had each other's back. One project kid is looking out for another.

On the other hand, if a family came into some good fortune, brutal criticism of their character would follow. People would say, "They always thought they were better!" when word spread that a family had bought a home and moved out of the project. Sarcasm was not always light-hearted either. If a person you didn't like had some unfortunate event, this would be followed by comments such as, "It's their own fault" or "They probably deserved what they got."

My friends and I quickly rebuked someone if anyone "spoke out of school" or did something foolish. We addressed a stupid comment or plan for what it was, and we spoke bluntly to each other. This directness translated into common sense street smarts that came in handy outside the project. But it did mean being guarded about your feelings. God forbid we would ever talk about feelings. Feelings were strictly off-limits unless you had had a few beers. If you did disclose and share some feelings, you had to be sure it could be brushed off as nothing but drunk talk the next day. Feelings and emotions were for sissies. Honestly, I don't know if this was something that immigrants brought with them from Ireland because discussing feelings was uncommon in our neighborhood of Irish immigrants. However, interactions with my friends were far more honest and direct than what was being discussed at home.

All kinds of characters lived in our housing development. The camaraderie was powerful because we shared the distinction of living in public housing. The most admired—the heroes—were the athletes. Everyone who played sports had a nickname that reflected some personal characteristic, and those were the stories most often told. I didn't have a nickname and did not want one, either. Two of my brothers had sports-related nicknames. These names were not flattering, and I never used their nickname to their face. (I'm not telling them here, either. You may ask them yourself!) To no one's surprise, being excellent in sports was the goal for most of us kids. You had a challenging life, subject to ridicule if you didn't play a sport.

Some guys excelled in sports, while others excelled in drinking alcohol. A handful pursued education, and the project was also home to lawyers, reporters, a couple of future priests, and many successful politicians. Former residents never forgot their roots and were always willing to help if someone needed a job or a few bucks. Many cops and firefighters also lived here, along with various utility workers, blue-collar workers, and criminals. We had truck hijackers, night-time burglars, jewelry store robbers, and even the notorious future FBI Most Wanted, James "Whitey" Bulger. His family also lived on Logan Way.

As his family and friends called him Jimmy, he was always good for a nickel or a dime if you ran into him in the project. Knowing Jimmy Bulger had other advantages, too, especially if you were going to get a beating from some other punk on the other side of South Boston. If someone threatened me or sensed a fight was coming, I would fabricate a story to say, "Do you know my Uncle Whitey? I'm supposed to meet him here tonight." Those words could work like magic to avoid an altercation.

Jimmy would also get me my first nightclub job, working the door at a club in downtown Boston. The legal drinking age in Massachusetts had just been changed to eighteen. I was a nineteen-year-old senior in high school when I ran into Jimmy and asked him if he knew anyone at the Kenmore Club in Boston.

"Why?" he asked.

"I'm going to apply for a job and just wanted to know if you knew anyone there," I said.

He said, "Go there and put in an application. Let me know how it goes."

I got the job.

I was attracted by the glamour, nightlife, and alcohol that came with working in one of the hottest clubs in Boston. The place was filled with wise guys and wannabe wise guys, and several were extremely dangerous characters.

I'm standing by the side door about three weeks into the job, ensuring no one got in without paying the cover charge, when Jim shows up at the nightclub. You could feel the tension rise in the wannabe wise guys hoping to shake Jim's hand and say hi when suddenly, Jim walks directly over to me and says, "Burkie, how's it going? Let's have a beer."

"Oh, jeez, Jim," I say. "We can't drink while working. I'll get in trouble."

"No," he says. "It's OK to have a beer."

"I appreciate that, Jim, but my manager will fire me if he sees me with a beer."

By now, the manager, bartenders, and other bouncers are huddled in a corner, talking to each other, wondering why Jim is talking to me.

"Where's the manager?" he asks.

I point to that group, "He's right over there."

"OK," Jim says, "I'll be right back."

All eyes are on Jim—the manager, the bartender, two waitresses, and some wannabe mafia guys in the corner—as he approaches the manager. I'm standing by the door thinking, *God, I hope he doesn't punch out the manager.*

The next thing I see, the manager nods, saying, "Yes, no problem, go ahead." Jim walks back over and says, "It's OK." Somehow, the manager of this exclusive nightclub violates the number one rule about drinking while on duty. Jimmy orders a couple of beers, and we stand there talking while most of my co-workers and the wise guys watch him.

Later that night, everyone comes over, wanting to know how I know Whitey. What am I going to say? That we lived in the same public housing project? So, I smile, laugh a little, and play it cute like we're close friends. I knew enough to keep my mouth shut and let them make assumptions. It's another example of one project person looking out for another.

Back at the project, everyone, except my Dad, got a good laugh when I told them what had happened. He did not think it was funny at all. He strongly advised me to quit the job immediately. He also gave me fatherly advice, "Listen to me," he said. "Don't ever get in a car with Jimmy. Take a taxi, a bus, or walk home." That was the end of the conversation. It seems my Dad had a certain intuition about Jim even back then. It would be many years later when the public became aware of all the crimes Jim had committed.

A Glass of Milk

"Write hard and clear about what hurts."
-Ernest Hemingway

One of our family traditions was Sunday dinner. We were like many other families in America, including the perfect television family, the Nelsons. Many families in America in those days were glued to the TV at least once a week to see what Ozzie and Harriet Nelson were up to in their safe and secure bucolic suburban home. The Nelson family handled difficulties with grace, wisdom, and dignity. What we had in common with the Nelsons was only that Sunday dinner. We sat down to eat at a specific time, said grace, and enjoyed a delicious meal prepared with love by Mom. Other than that, our family could not be confused with life on American TV shows. The healthy and functional life of the Nelsons was not the way we lived in our home.

On a typical Sunday, we would all be at the table waiting for Dad to return home from the noon Mass. Sometimes, one or two of us boys would attend services with him, but not always. When I did, I sat on the other side of the church with my friends. When Dad got back from church, Mom would serve the meal. It was frequently roast beef with potatoes, green vegetables, and bread and butter. The bread was always a loaf of Wonder Bread, still in the package.

We would start by saying grace and thanking God for the delicious dinner. Then, we would always call out to see who would get the favorite end piece of the roast. The argument could get heated, but Mom always resolved the problem by cutting off both ends of the roast and cutting them into pieces so we could each enjoy it a little bit.

Family meals are among my most vivid memories. Roast Beef on Sunday. Franks and beans, with brown bread on Saturdays. Pasta, meatloaf, tuna fish sandwiches, or leftovers on the other days of the week. On Fridays during Lent, it seemed the entire neighborhood abstained from eating meat and instead had fish. We ate according to my father's work schedule, with dinner at five o'clock every day, except on Sundays when it was always one o'clock on the dot.

One particular Sunday, when I was about nine years old, is imprinted in my mind. On this day, Dad had worked in the firehouse the night before. He comes home around eight this morning. As we did every week, we sat down to Sunday dinner at one o'clock and said grace. Dad had a drink in front of him. Usually, I just had a glass of water with dinner, but on this day, I feel especially hungry, and the delicious roast beef aroma permeating the whole house makes me even more anxious to eat. I am so rushed to sit down that I don't grab my usual glass of water. Instead, one of my brothers fills my glass (which in its previous life had been a small grape jelly jar) with milk. Unlike my brothers, who all enjoy a cold glass of milk, I prefer water.

I casually say, "Brian can have my milk. I'm going to get some water." As I sheepishly push away from the table, I hear a deep voice say, "Just sit down and drink the milk like everyone else." For some reason, I feel an uneasy sense of dread that I have never experienced before. *It's best not to argue.* I ignore the milk.

About halfway through dinner, my father ordered me to drink the milk again. Maybe he feels I should be grateful to have milk because he works two jobs to put food on the table. But his tone frightens me.

"I don't like milk," I protest.

Mom says, "Oh, Tim, just drink the milk like your brothers."

"But I don't like milk." The taste, the texture—nothing about it appeals to me. Seeing my brothers drink milk from the carton makes me gag.

"Drink the goddamn milk," shouts Dad. "Drink it. You are not leaving this table until you drink it."

"I don't like milk," I say, tears welling up while a huge, painful lump forms in my throat. "I don't like the taste." I just want some water.

"DRINK IT!"

"Come on, Tim," says one of my brothers, attempting to cheer me on.

"Go ahead, Tim. Look how easy it goes down," says another.

Yet another brother offered to drink the milk for me, but Dad's voice only got louder. "DRINK THE DAMN MILK!" He takes a sip of his whiskey and gives me an angry stare.

By this time, I am crying and pleading. "Please, Dad, please don't make me drink the milk. I don't like it. I can't stand the taste. I cannot drink it. Please don't make me drink it."

Tension and silence join us at the dinner table.

Finally, Mom says quietly, "John, he doesn't want it."

"I don't care. He is going to drink it."

The world begins to close in on me. I place the glass to my lips and manage to drink some of it. After that, I can't eat anything, leaving the prize-winning piece of roast beef untouched on my plate. I just want to get away. I make a final attempt to take another sip of milk, but I can't control myself and spit it out. It's not an ordinary spit, but a heaving retch with milk flowing out of the side of my mouth. I put the glass down and cry, "I tried, I tried to drink it, I tried. I couldn't swallow it." Dad ordered me to leave the table.

This was the first time I experienced another side of my Dad—a strange and terrifying side. My invincible fire-fighting hero had another side to him that frightened me. Also, this was my first opportunity to be the scapegoat. I believe that several of my brothers had the unfortunate experience of being the family scapegoat many times over the next few years.

Dad didn't win, and neither did I. This incident was the first of many painful and disappointing altercations with Dad. As the tension built up, the lump in my throat felt so large and painful that it nearly blocked my ability to talk or cry. There was so much fear at the table that this changed my perception of Dad.

It is true that on many occasions, we enjoyed a family dinner with conversation, community, and love. But the glass of whiskey on the table was an ever-present distraction, and I would look around, wondering which way it would go, how it would end. *Where is that glass of whiskey going to take us tonight?*

Timothy to Thomas

At least once and sometimes twice a month, we visited our Uncle Thomas and Aunt Teresa, my mother's brother and his wife. It was a short thirty-minute ride to their house in Milton, a suburb of Boston. Uncle Tom and Aunt Teresa were exceedingly kind and generous to us kids. They had no kids and lovingly treated us as their surrogate children. I especially enjoyed seeing them and their beautiful German Shepherd dogs. We never had a dog growing up because dog ownership violated the rules of the project. The first one I remember was Trinka, and when he passed, their next dog was named Blitzen, after the reindeer. I had so much fun playing with the dogs, exploring the neighborhood, and walking in the green space and nearby woods.

The adults sat around and chatted, always with drinks, while we kids enjoyed unlimited soda and snacks. The conversation sometimes led to my Uncle Tom providing some entertainment for all. After a few drinks, he would put on his amateur show, singing along to records and encouraging us to join him. Once, I recited a poem and was rewarded with a five-dollar bill—a significant amount of money, although not enough to coax this shy boy to become a regular performer like my Mom and younger brothers.

Uncle Tom had a vivid imagination. He often donned a giant sombrero, draped a colorful poncho over his shoulders, and wore a stick-on mustache while speaking with a fake Mexican accent. He told us stories about an Indian tribe with a chief named Dimitris living nearby in the Blue Hills. We never met Chief Dimitris, but courtesy of Uncle Tom and Aunt Teresa, we received gifts from Dimitris every Christmas and on our birthdays, including winter jackets, Indian blankets, candy, and silver dollars. One Christmas, my brothers and I kept hounding my uncle, demanding to know when we could finally meet Chief Dimitris. Where was he? Why couldn't he be here? Uncle Tom announced, straight-faced, "Dimitris is in Miami for the winter…but he sends his regards."

That silver dollar tradition continues today. John, my eldest brother, gives all the great-nieces and nephews a silver dollar from Dimitris every Christmas until they graduate from college. Like Uncle Tom, he encourages the kids to sing or recite poems. Several of our nephews and nieces have saved all their silver dollars from Dimitris, a significant collection of coins they promise to hand down to their kids. It wasn't until I was much older that I learned Dimitris was a Greek name. It was comical to think Uncle Tom picked a Greek name for a native American.

Almost all these visits were terrific. However, in one incident the same year, Dad insisted I drink the milk and told a different story. In addition to us, friends of Uncle Tom's were visiting, so the party was a little larger and a little more boisterous than usual. All of us kids were wrestling on the floor, playing with Trinka, and, in general, having a ball. We wished we could ride the dog, but we were too big for that, so my Dad offered each of us "horseback rides."

He gets down on all fours and gives each kid a short horseback ride through the recreation area in the basement, maneuvering around the ping-pong table and some bar stools. Kids being kids, between the ages of 8-10 years, we start getting rambunctious, pushing and shoving to be the next in line for a ride. I'm hanging on my father's back when someone tries to push me off. I continue to hang on and fight for my spot, and someone's knees come down on Dad's back. Understandably upset, he says, "That's it. No more rides. You guys are too rough."

I fall over and lay on the floor half under the ping-pong table, laughing, thinking this is great fun. Then, for some unknown reason, I sensed my Dad becoming angrier. Feeling it best to retreat a little, I slide farther under the table to escape him and the other kids. That's when he reaches under the ping-pong table, pulls me toward him, and grasps the back of my calf. It feels like getting caught in the bear trap I saw on TV. I cry out, and he pulls me closer, saying, "Don't you ever do that again."

I can't help reacting, "That hurts! I didn't do anything." This angers him more, and I can feel his grip tighten. His fingers dig into the back of my calf, and pain shoots up my leg. He pulls me closer, looks directly into my eyes, and repeats, "Don't you ever do that again." He is furious at all of us, but his anger is directed at me, the scapegoat again.

I am inches away from him, smelling the whiskey on his breath. He repeats his warning and adds, "I'll give you something to cry about." I am tearing up and saying I'm sorry. He releases his grip, and I retreat farther under the table, trying to hide. I stayed there for what seemed to be an eternity until my uncle came over and asked if I was all right. He then asks if I can help him move the lawnmower in the backyard before it gets dark. He reaches under the table for my hand and carefully helps me stand. We walk out to the yard together, but the lawnmower isn't there. He suddenly remembers putting it away earlier and hands me a one-dollar bill. He says, "Here. This is for being so kind and offering to help me today. Buy yourself an ice cream."

He asks if I will stay back in the yard and play with the German Shepherd, Trinka, until he "does his duty" and then bring him in after he finishes. I'm happy to stay outside with the dog until it's time to go home. We load the car for a long, silent, uncomfortable trip back to the project. I feel frightened and nauseous, recalling the whiskey on my Dad's breath the entire ride home. Dad and Mom are oblivious to my feelings and talk about how much fun they had with Tom and Teresa. I sit silently for the remainder of the ride, hoping to get to bed without another incident.

Dad had taken the joy out of visiting Tom and Teresa, especially when the alcohol started to flow. I now had to be on guard to prepare myself for another of my father's outbursts. That emotionally painful experience was cataloged in my brain, along with several more over the next few years. Dad's dark, intoxicated side would suddenly reappear, and I would realize he could not be trusted because he unexpectedly changed into someone other than my loving and invincible Dad.

The day after the horseback ride incident, my teacher gave our class a simple penmanship assignment. I completed it and wrote my name on my paper as Thomas Burke. Of course, the teacher noticed and reminded me my name was Timothy.

I did not want to be Timothy. I wanted to be Thomas, a kind and loving person like my Uncle Tom.

"No," she said. "You must write Timothy on the line for your name, not Thomas." We went back and forth until she informed me that if I did not write my real name, she would tell my mother, who would then tell my father.

The third-grade teacher won the battle, and I continued using Timothy. It was too difficult to explain why I wanted to change it. The truth is, at this young age, I did not like myself and wanted to be anyone other than me.

Growing Up Hard and Fast

Although we did not understand the concepts or dynamics of emotional trauma, we knew every time a kid went "berserk," we dared not push his buttons. "Going berserk" was another way of saying that a kid had a meltdown, lacked adequate coping skills, and had difficulty regulating emotions. They probably had pent-up frustrations and a limited range to express their feelings, which accurately described many of us kids in the neighborhood. We knew a kid could take only so much abuse, only so much pressure, before he would explode, yelling and screaming and letting it all out. It's just a typical meltdown. Sometimes, it manifested in a kid picking up a rock or a brick to throw at a moving vehicle or someone's head. I witnessed this on several occasions. Fistfights, joy rides in stolen cars, wrecked cars, arson, theft, and general violence were common in the Southie projects. The neighborhood was very active and, at times, dangerously volatile.

I entered a newspaper distribution shop two blocks from the project one Saturday morning. Two guys working there were much older and bigger than me. They started teasing me about my grubby clothing and sneakers, calling me a "dirt ball from the project." We didn't wear socks and wore the same sneakers all summer, so our feet did get dirty and smelly those days. I recall wearing my sneakers until they had holes in the bottom of them. Just like many other kid's sneakers had back then. Many people believe Project Kids are disreputable rejects. I was accustomed to hearing that, but this time, it bothered me. I felt angry, so I walked outside the shop to get away. To my left were some windows along the storefront. I kicked two windows, and my rage was so intense that one direct kick caused each window to explode, shattering the glass. The two guys and the store owner ran out to see what had happened.

As they assessed the damage, they were shocked and confused that a preteen could quickly produce so much destruction. I'm sure they wanted to smack me, but I was too young. As I started to walk away casually toward the project, the owner informed me that I was barred from the store and was never to return. Prior experience had taught me that outsiders wouldn't chase you into the projects because they would be outnumbered and would have to deal with the friends who would protect me. I looked over my shoulder and said to him, "Drop dead, ya mothah fuckah!" I must admit that my going berserk gave me a strange sense of power.

Everyone had an outlet—participating in sports, fighting, drinking, romancing, risk-taking, making music, or going berserk if no other outlet was available. A person saying or doing the wrong thing could quickly get punched in the face or, worse, hit with a bottle or stick over the head. Anything might be the wrong thing to say or do on the right day. Sometimes, friends would jump into the fray to limit the damage. Other times, you might sit back and enjoy the show.

Living in the projects, we became hardened, streetwise kids early on. We sometimes resembled the young pickpockets in Dickens's novel *Oliver Twist*. We didn't need a Fagin to show us how to operate and survive. When strangers or outsiders entered the neighborhood, we felt they violated our space. We banded together and carefully observed them. We could tell when an unknown visitor at the neighbor's place was a bill collector demanding an installment payment for some debt. At the age of ten, I could look people in the eye and lie very convincingly. I knew exactly what to say when any outsider asked if a neighbor was home: "No, I haven't seen her all day," was the standard answer, even if we knew Mrs. O'Leary had been hanging out her laundry five minutes earlier. After the bill collector left, we would report to Mrs. O'Leary that some man was looking for her. The word also spread quickly if a doctor or, heaven forbid, the parish priest appeared. People would assume something was wrong in that house, and the gossip would gallop throughout the project. We were a very pessimistic community.

As kids, we mastered foul language like longshoremen working on a dock. I could swear in Polish, too! If an unsuspecting adult—one not from the project—reprimanded one of us, the response was a barrage of f-bombs and other jargon that would make a drill sergeant blush. The look of shock on their faces was always entertaining to observe. We wouldn't dare use profanity on adults who lived in the project because they likely knew who we were and would tell our parents. And we knew that would have consequences.

Every day among my friends, you could hear a string of common disparaging epithets and derogatory phrases. Often, it seemed this was the extent of our vocabulary. When we were older, sitting at the bar, we'd still say to each other at least fifty times a night, "Shut the fuck up," or "I'll fuckin' kill you!" If someone missed the opportunity to score during a football game or didn't live up to other expectations or community standards, we'd curse them out. There was little empathy from this crowd. Everyone was treated the same, and you were called out for your mistakes, or in our vernacular, for your bullshit. The exception was if you were an athlete. Then, the neighborhood commentators always gave you a pass. Respect and support for the much-admired athletes must be preserved, it seemed.

You had to constantly prove to yourself and anyone else you didn't deserve a gay slur or to be cursed out as a coward. This might mean fighting, destroying something, or even hitting an innocent bystander. If you appeared crazy, it was better than being branded a coward. It is impossible to know how often someone said to me, "I'll kill you!" or "Shut the fuck up!" It was just how emotions were handled in my neighborhood—direct and right to the point.

We also knew how to throw a sucker punch before one came our way. I recall playing outside with my brother and some friends when an older boy came walking over, who had picked on me days before. Knowing my brother was standing nearby, I took this opportunity to call this kid out. Earlier that day, he had had ear surgery and was wearing a large bandage on his left ear. I stood up to him and yelled at him for picking on me. He was standing there taking my verbal abuse with one eye fixed on my big brother, realizing he might be fighting the two of us. I swung at him, landing my closed fist on his ear with the bandage. He went down and screamed in pain, and everyone was shocked at what I had just done. The other kids couldn't believe it. I hit him dead center in the bandage over his wound. He slowly got up, and before he could swing at me, my brother stepped in and told him to go home. He also told me to go home. I spent the next year looking over my shoulder, waiting for this kid to pounce on me, but it never happened.

You had to appear tough in the project or risk getting targeted and picked on. There were many opportunities to get picked on or abused. When I was thirteen, a parish priest put his hand on my leg while I sat in his car. He was expecting something different from me when I said, "Remove your hand, or I will Effing stab you." The conversation abruptly ended. I got out of his car at the next light and walked home. He avoided making eye contact whenever we crossed paths in the neighborhood.

However, over the years, I did not allow this incident to discourage or deter me from interacting and seeking assistance from various compassionate and supportive religious individuals, including several priests. I was fair-minded and thought it best not to judge all priests and paint them with the same brush due to the actions of one sinister person.

I knew of incidents of sexual abuse perpetrated on several kids in our community, including me. I will spare you the details. Living in family dysfunction during our teenage years is difficult enough, but this difficulty becomes compounded when you include sexual abuse into the equation. Like all my problems, trauma, and anxieties, I categorized, compartmentalized, and buried them deep within myself. It wasn't until many years later that I was able to address this issue because, at that time, I had more pressing problems in my life to worry about.

Looking back, I can see the extent of my desensitization as a young adult. I recall when one of our friends got his first apartment in Dorchester. He had a big party where there was plenty of alcohol and weed. I was standing in the kitchen with a small group of people when a guy walked in waving a small handgun. He was showing off, and nobody was impressed or frightened of this idiot.

Suddenly, the gun went off, and we all froze for a minute. The guy standing beside me, also leaning on the stove, lifted his shirt to examine himself. He sees that he has been shot in the belly, turns to me, and says, "I've been shot." I see the bullet wound and say, "No shit Sherlock." "You'd better get to the hospital." Instead of calling an ambulance, the other guys said, "Don't call the cops. They'll break up the party." "Someone called him a cab." Two guys escorted him to the hospital while the remaining group continued partying into the night. He survived. No big deal was our attitude.

Most of my friend's parents played "the number." This was illegal gambling in poor and working-class neighborhoods before the establishment of the state lottery. The number would appear in the afternoon paper, the third column of numbers. Three down and one to the left. It was common for adults to ask us, kids, if we knew today's number. It was the talk of the neighborhood if someone hit "the number." I only had one friend, Richard, whose father hit the number and used the money to purchase a house. He was one wise man.

My friends and I often delivered bets to the local bookie for our parents as a regular chore. My mother would have me run an "errand" to Bill the Bookie. She wrote down her number on a piece of paper and folded it so it could hold a dime or quarter. I was to take it across the street to Bill's Barber Shop, operated by none other than Bill the Bookie. Bill would be cutting hair as I walked in. He would see me out of the corner of his eye and call me over as he put his hand by his side. I slyly hand him the folded paper and say, "This is from my mother." Bill would place it in his pocket and return to cutting hair without missing a beat. I still play my mother's lucky number on her birthday every year, but her number had never hit for the past fifty years when I played it.

Most of my friends' parents drank alcohol frequently and often to excess. It was common in the project to see a friend's mom, dad, or my parents walk home impaired, staggering, falling down drunk. Alcohol was ubiquitous at neighborhood parties and the Fourth of July cookouts that we called "weenie roasts." Most families on the block would pull out a grill and start cooking hotdogs and hamburgers, washed down with soda for kids and plenty of alcohol for the adults. Each courtyard hosted its little block party to celebrate the Fourth with the neighbors.

As we got older, the "weenie roast" evolved into the annual July 4th BASH, complete with eighty to ninety cases of beer, plenty of hard liquor, food, and music. Someone figured out that buying beer and bottles of liquor in tax-free New Hampshire would be cheaper, so each year, the guys would rent a truck to make the trip across the state line. In addition, a raffle was held each hour of the day, and the prize was one ounce of marijuana. There was always a large group of young (underage) people drinking, and nobody enforced the drinking age. The partying continued into the night until all the alcohol and weed were gone. The July 4th BASH was the highlight of the summer. Each year, on July 4th, I show a film clip of the event for all my friends to enjoy.

It was common to see adults sitting in small groups outside during summer, chatting and enjoying a few beers. My parents drank as much, if not more, than other parents, and I recognized early that my father tended to drink more than everyone. He preferred whiskey, but he was not one to turn down a cold beer.

When we were hanging on the corner, my friends and I often saw one of our parents stagger by, drunk. We all knew it could easily be our dad or mom walking by and embarrassing us in front of our friends. Most kids had the same experience of having a parent who drank too much. Most came from difficult homes, but we never let our friends see the pain we felt about that. Often, someone would change the subject or make a joke and move on while their parents walked home. Primarily, our reaction was to be silent and let them pass. We never wanted to be the kid known for his parent's drunkenness.

I vividly remember all the details when I witnessed a family experiencing the shame and trauma of public intoxication one summer afternoon. I looked on in shock as this event unfolded, focusing on the question: *Could this ever be my dad and me?* Based on our family history, I believed this was inevitable, which frightened me.

Two young kids, Billy and Stanley, from the neighborhood had to go into a bar to bring their dad home. Their dad was escorted and physically thrown out of the barroom in the center of Andrew Square, which is not far from our house. Their father was a professional boxer and a barroom brawler. Everyone knows Mr. Polanski is one tough street-fighting man and a heavy drinker. His scarred face, broken nose, and "cauliflower ears" from the fights he participated in mark him as a brawler not to be challenged or toyed with.

He is highly intoxicated and fights with another man in the barroom when he is thrown out onto the sidewalk. He tries to stand, yelling about wanting another drink. His shirt is partially torn, and wet urine stains his pants. His ten and twelve-year-old boys come to the barroom to fetch him home. Going to the bar to retrieve one's father is not uncommon in our community or unfamiliar to many kids.

One of the boys, Billy, is in my class at the local grammar school. I watch in shock as he and his younger brother, Stanley, plead with their dad to go home. "Please, Dad, come home," they cry out. Their dad struggles to stand as he yells for the bartender, "Come out and fight like a man!" These two sobbing young boys plead for this to stop as they continue trying their best to defuse the situation, hanging onto their dad's waist as he struggles to gain his balance. The alcoholic in him, intoxicated and full of bravado, insists on continuing the fight, demanding that he not be "shut off" and instead that he be let back into the bar room.

A short time later, their mother shows up and adds her voice, begging her husband to go home and sleep it off. The crowd looks on as the drunken dad pushes the mom down to the sidewalk. The boys scream in pain and shame at what they and the world are witnessing.

My friend Billy glances into my eyes as he struggles to grasp this embarrassing, hurtful, and untenable situation. I look at him for a split second and feel his shame as we both turn to avoid any semblance of knowing each other. I sense he wants this to end as much as I do. But I also feel this could be me. I believe it's only a matter of time before this will be me. I'm so full of fear, shock, and sadness as I observe the humiliation that this family is experiencing. I'm vicariously living that experience through Billy. I have an ominous feeling that this will be my brothers and me bringing our dad home from the barroom someday.

Several TV shows we watched as kids always seemed to have a drunkard in the storyline. Usually, the drunk character was funny and often not too harmful to themselves. I often watched the *Andy Griffith Show* to see the town drunk, Otis, turn himself in and lock himself up in jail. Elsewhere, Dean Martin frequently imbibed while singing while holding a cigarette in his hand. Foster Brooks made a career of portraying a lovable drunk. *The Red Skelton Show* featured many drunks in the entertainment world. Similarly, in *The Honeymooners* with Jackie Gleason, drunks were in the plot lines. I enjoyed many of these shows, but I never observed a raging alcoholic terrorize his family on TV.

The attractive side of drinking was also emphasized in popular songs of that time: "Show Me the Way To Go Home," "99 Bottles of Beer on the Wall," "There Lays the Glass," and "The Parting Glass." Not even poetry was immune. "The Face on the Barroom Floor" was a widely recited poem back then. I memorized much of it as a child.

It seemed alcohol was everywhere I turned. It looked glamorous and fun when we watched the adults drinking, dancing, and singing at parties. I wanted to emulate them. It seemed natural that when the opportunity came to socialize like our parents—with alcohol—we would do the same. And we did. Most of my friends began their drinking as very young teenagers. My friends and I often joked that the legal drinking age in the housing project was thirteen.

We also "socialized" in other ways that were not conducive to peace and quiet but were illegal and dangerous. For example, when one of the older guys stole a car or "hotbox," as we called it, it was common to "dump it" or leave it in the middle of one of the many project courtyards. This was an invitation for us younger kids to break the windows and light the car on fire. I participated in several of these demolitions and saw many stolen vehicles torched. I also recall praying as a burning car went up in flames that my father's fire truck would not be the one to show up to extinguish the fire.

When I was around eleven or twelve, one of my buddies was standing on the hood of a "hotbox" that had been abandoned near my house. He smashed a rock through the front windshield, making a massive crash. I walked over and struck a wooden match over the open gas tank. I dropped the lit match, and the flame that jumped up and out made a loud whoosh. Some of the older guys were playing basketball nearby, and a guy named Joe, a friend of my older brother, grabbed me from behind and pulled me away.

"Are you freakin' crazy?" he yelled.

This type of disregard for safety and risk-taking was sometimes encouraged among my peers. Still, if the older guys had gone through similar situations and possibly witnessed friends injured, you might get a stern warning or a kick in the ass. Fortunately, the tank was empty, and only the fumes ignited. To this day, when Joe sees me, he's not shy in reminding me I was "the luckiest bastard in the project."

Another time, a friend and I attempted to climb a chain-link fence to hop on a freight train for a joyride. The metal fence, intended to separate the project from the railroad tracks, was fifteen feet high, with sharp barbed wire running along the top. This was designed to prevent exactly what we were trying to do. I had one arm over the top when I slipped and fell. The underside of my arm was torn wide open. Blood was everywhere. With a look of terror, my buddy said, "You better get home," and promptly disappeared. I picked myself up off the ground and walked home alone, crying. When my Mom saw the large, open wound and the exposed muscle and bone, she called the police. A Boston cop named Charlie, who knew our family, arrived quickly, took one look at my arm, placed a dirty dish towel over the wound, and ordered my mother: "Throw him in the back of the cruiser." We drove to the Boston City Hospital emergency room with the siren screaming and the lights flashing. The doctors told my Mom they would try to save my arm. It took forty-five stitches to sew up the wound. I thought I was the cat's ass that summer and showed everyone my scar like a medal of honor. I proudly proclaimed that I got it trying to climb over the fence to hop a freight train!

Public housing projects in Southie were also an excellent marketplace for stolen goods. There were plenty of thieves, and you could tell when someone's father or uncle had "hit a truck" because they suddenly appeared with new leather shoes and a new leather jacket.

A wide variety of items were prone to be stolen and resold, such as records (usually 45 RPMs because they were small enough to stuff down the front of your pants), sporting equipment, portable tape players, 8-track tapes, car radios, shoes, and scally caps. The most prized item was a leather jacket. Many of my friends and I had full-length Spanish leather jackets. We purchased them from a local thief from the project who also drove a taxi. I told my parents that one of my buddies had loaned me the coat because "It didn't fit him, and he couldn't return it." On one occasion, eight of us showed up at the same barroom wearing our full-length leather coats. It looked like a (stolen) leather jacket convention.

My Mom did her best to instill values in us because she did not want her children to be thieves or thugs. When I was eleven, she caught me stealing from the Five and Dime store across the street from our house. I accompanied her to the store, and while she was talking with the owner, I placed a toy in my pocket when no one was watching. It was a small, colorful pinwheel with a plunger that produced sparks as it spun around. I thought that it was very cool.

As we walked home, I pulled out the toy and started to watch the sparks fly and the colorful pinwheel spin. Mom looked and asked me where I had gotten that. I pointed at the Five and Dime and smiled. She firmly scolded me, telling me it was not right to steal and that I would have to return it. She marched me back to the store to return the item to the owner. The three of us stood there, and my Mom asked me, "Do you have something to say to Max?" At first, I said I had found this toy and wanted to return it, but Mom said, "No, you took it and want to apologize and return it." I apologized and handed him the toy. Max was serious but kind, as he taught me the importance of not stealing. I was embarrassed as we walked home in silence. I could feel Mom's disappointment in me. I was grateful she didn't tell my father. Lesson learned.

In general, stealing wasn't my thing. Unless, of course, it was too good of an opportunity. When I was fifteen years old, I went downtown with a friend, intending to steal a few records. Joey and I visited a large department store to check out the new 45 RPMs. We were getting ready to make our move when we noticed the store detective watching us and preparing to close in. Joey told me to stand in front of him to block the detective's view. Joey was holding four records, and, in a flash, he put two of them down the front of his pants and pulled his T-shirt over the top. He held the remaining records for the detective to see and placed them back on the rack. We continued to meander around the record department for a few minutes before heading to the exit door. The detective suddenly appeared out of nowhere, blocking our path, while a second man stood behind us. Trapped! I thought we would be arrested when the detective said, "Lucky you returned those records. I was about to arrest you and take you two to the juvenile court."

Joey and I walked outside as the detective watched us through the large front display window. Joey banged on the display window with his fist, pulled the two records out from his pants, waved them at the man, and yelled, "Thanks a lot, sucker!"

The stunned detective started running toward the door. Joey handed me one of the records, and we ran as fast as possible to catch the next train back to the project. It was a bit of a close call, but it did not deter us from returning a month later for more records.

Big John

My father's start in life was not an easy one. He was born in 1918, the year of the Spanish Flu pandemic. Death was everywhere at that time. His mother lost her husband, brother, and father in one week, becoming a widow with two children. Dad was only six months old. She never remarried and raised my Dad and his older brother as a single mom. Dad lived through the Great Depression and enlisted in the Navy during World War II, serving on a ship in the South Pacific. He met my Mom in Boston's Hyde Park High School, and they married before he shipped out to sea. After the war, they moved into a small apartment in the Old Harbor Project in South Boston, along with many other veterans. He studied The Red Book for the firefighter's exam and became a member of the Boston Fire Department in January 1947. He was assigned to Ladder 13 in the South End neighborhood of Boston.

Dad's nickname was Big John. My oldest brother was also named John. My Mom called them Big John and Little John. But Dad was large and robust in stature, so friends and co-workers called him Big John for that reason. He was just as in the song Jimmy Dean sang, "…wide at the shoulders and narrow at the hip, and everyone knows you don't give any lip to Big John." Those words were a fact of life in our home, not just song lyrics. As a child, I felt safe and loved by the big guy until I didn't. Dad was six feet two inches tall, 235 pounds, had a thirty-eight-inch waist, and was naturally muscular.

Being a Boston firefighter was difficult enough, but with a wife and six boys, the extra income was necessary to pay all the bills, so Dad found a second part-time job as a truck driver. His natural strength was further developed by manually loading and unloading construction materials by hand from the back of the flatbed truck. He had large hands, and his friends and coworkers nicknamed him "cement hands."

Dad set specific rules in our house for us to follow. One such rule was that "Burke boys were good boys." Whenever my parents asked us, "What are Burke boys?" in front of relatives or their friends, we had to say "good boys" and say it with a smile. My Dad would proudly say, "Very good. Yes, Burke boys are good boys." This was interesting because as I got older, sometimes the family motto felt like a threat.

He also taught us to look someone in the eye while properly shaking their hand—always a firm handshake. You remembered Big John when he shook your hands because of his eye contact, firm grip, and large, strong hand. It was a fundamental value for him that we always acted like gentlemen and never brought shame to this family.

Another rule was never to use the "N" word, the "F" word, or any other foul language in our home. (Outside the house was different. The N-word was part of our vocabulary.) If we forgot and let it slip out, my parents reprimanded us quickly. My Dad never used the "N" word, which was commonly heard on the street and in the project at that time. Racism was rampant in Boston in that era. My Dad's firehouse was in the South End of Boston, a predominantly poor Black neighborhood. He was keenly aware of the widespread poverty and substandard living conditions, and he respected his many friends in that community. He enjoyed meeting black and white people in the neighborhood and could converse with anyone. Regarding people skills, he was a patient man and a good listener.

Throughout my life, I repeatedly heard people say what a great guy Big John Burke was. People who saw the outside of our home saw a Boston firefighter who worked hard at two jobs and went to church on Sunday. They saw a father of six boys, a man with a pleasant demeanor who always had something nice to say. What's not to love?

Dad's firehouse district was one of the busiest in Boston. His job was Tillerman—the man who sits on the back of a hook-and-ladder truck and steers the rear wheels. Having a tillerman allows a big ladder truck to navigate the narrow streets and tight corners often found in cities. The Tillerman must be vigilant for changes in traffic conditions or obstructions and has to coordinate his steering with the driver's lead, often at high speeds, as the truck rushes to battle a fire.

Sitting at the tiller wheel also meant being exposed to the elements. During the winter, Dad was routinely battered by rain, snow, and sleet. The reward for having the tillerman position was usually the first up the ladder into the burning building or onto the roof to start cutting holes to release the smoke.

Many dinner conversations were about Dad's day at work fighting fires. His stories of fires and rescues were captivating. He was often exhausted after battling fires and was welcomed home as our hero. We asked him about the news reports of fires he'd fought, destroyed buildings and the injuries and deaths he witnessed.

But heroism came with a price. We saw firsthand what exposure to fire and smoke could do to a person. In those days, firefighting equipment was not nearly as effective or sophisticated as it is today. The building and fire safety codes, including sprinkler system requirements, didn't exist as they do today. Many of the older buildings around Boston were wooden and structurally dangerous. Fires often resulted in out-of-control conflagrations that these men were required to enter. Firefighters did not have an oxygen tank backpack but a simple mask with a filter to protect them from inhaling smoke and chemicals. Bloodshot eyes, cuts, bruises, and other injuries were part of the job. Dad's sinuses were often filled with black sooty residue, and it would take him several hours of coughing and nose-blowing to get some relief. The persistent smell of smoke permeated his body, hair, and clothing. Mom often suggested he shower before dinner, even though he had already showered and changed clothes at the firehouse before coming home.

It seemed as though Dad shook off all these difficulties. I never once heard him complain about the challenges of his job. As we Burke boys witnessed every day, he always credited the brave efforts of his brother firefighters while minimizing the risk involved in the battle. All these men would do all this and more, then return to work the next day to do it again without complaining or seeking accolades.

As I write about my childhood experiences, I feel ambivalent and conflicted. My Mom always said, "You never repeat what you heard in the kitchen." Loyalty was expected from each of us. It seemed like the entire neighborhood was in on this. The "Golden Rule" was expected and admired in the community, and anything other than that was wrong. If you spoke "out of school," you were considered a "rat bastard" or traitor. The expectation always was that you suck it up and move on. I can hear the voices of some of the old timers from Ireland saying, "Jesus, Mary, and Joseph. You don't speak publicly about family matters, for fook's sake! Buck up! Just buck up and move along!"

Believe me when I tell you I am conflicted as I write about my childhood experiences. However, silence and denial did not help me as a child. I decided to tell my story because of the importance of being true to myself and my desire for the truth to help another child of an alcoholic or a recovering alcoholic.

From a very young age, I was aware that my father's drinking was something to be concerned about, and even more so after the time he insisted I drink milk with Sunday dinner. I knew when he was drinking and when he was not—it was never a gray area. When my father drank alcohol, he had a consistent and profound personality change. His facial expression changed dramatically and was immediately noticeable. He had a blank look in his eyes—often referred to as the "hundred-mile stare." When I saw this, I wondered *where did my Dad go?* His speaking voice changed to a low, direct monotone, which was often slowed and, at times, slurring. He often appeared lethargic but also angry. I have rarely seen this dramatic change in other active alcoholics. Still, as a kid, when I noticed this personality change, I would avoid verbal or physical contact for fear of setting off this intoxicated stranger who lived in my house. I learned to be on guard if I could smell the whiskey on his breath when I gave him a kiss, hello, or goodbye. I remained vigilant even when he was not home, cowering with anticipation about what could happen when he returned home—anticipating each potential traumatic scene in my head.

During the summer, the combined odor of alcohol and sweat made him smell like a piece of red meat going rancid. It not only indicated that he was drinking but also spoke of what was to come. Arguing, yelling, accusations, threats, tension, fear, and shame could soon fill the room. Or not. There was always uncertainty present. The "here and now" for me was filled with fear and confusion. There was so much fear that it spilled into my future thoughts. I sometimes believed it would always be like this, which was disheartening.

We never seemed to know what would precipitate an outburst from Dad or when a simple disagreement would turn into a severe shouting match. Once again, it could have been the booze talking. An unbalanced checkbook, a cold dinner, dishes in the sink, and hockey equipment not put away could be the spark that lit the fuse. Sometimes, Dad would pass out on the sofa, and thankfully, there wouldn't be an argument that night.

I knew that my parents loved each other. They were often affectionate, and when Dad came home from the firehouse or his second job delivering construction supplies, they greeted each other with a hug and a kiss and exchanged compliments. They enjoyed each other's company at parties and other social events. They had a powerful love for each other and saw beyond their faults. I often received compliments about them and how they were a lovely, attractive couple. A neighbor once told me they were the best-looking couple in South Boston.

For the most part, my parents went to bed each evening without any confrontation. Other times, they would argue about something stupid or a minor misunderstanding from earlier in the evening, and it would start all over again. The shouting, shoving, name-calling, and insanity would disrupt the household. We just lay in our beds in fear until the yelling stopped, and it was safe to fall asleep.

Like many families in the project, our family lived paycheck to paycheck. My mother drove to the firehouse each Thursday afternoon to pick up my Dad's weekly salary. Often, my younger brothers and I would tag along. She couldn't wait to get the check, cash it, and go food shopping. Getting that paycheck also prevented Dad from spending it on alcohol.

On one of these firehouse visits, I realized Dad's drinking was a real problem inside and outside our home. He and his fellow firefighters sat on a bench outside the firehouse, waiting for the alarm to ring, drinking alcohol from brown paper bags. When Mom pulled up, she could immediately tell what was happening. I could also see that things were not right.

"For Christ's sake, you're drinking? It's the middle of the day! What the hell is wrong with you guys? Someone is going to get killed," she said.

One of the guys responded, "Calm down, Patricia. It's okay. We're fine."

"Bullshit! Look at you!" she shouted. "I'm going to tell the Commissioner!"

The officer of the day came out of the station house with the paycheck.

"One of these guys will get killed, and it's your fault!" she said.

"Take it easy, Pat," he said. "They're off duty soon. Here's the paycheck."

I'll never forget that incident and how it changed my perception of my father and his heroic brother firefighters. He was not only drinking at home but also at work. The shiny red trucks, the paper bags, the boisterous laughter, the fear in my mother's eyes, and the resignation in the officer's voice indicated something was not right. I was surprised and concerned, but I wasn't quite sure what it all meant.

This routine of picking up the weekly paycheck was repeated many times during my childhood. Mom genuinely feared that one of the firefighters would get hurt or die while fighting a fire because of their alcohol abuse. One of the men had the audacity to say, "Jesus Christ, John, what's wrong with Pat?" Mom was angry, but she tried not to show it.

Growing up, one thing that was always present was fear—the anticipation of impending doom. The atmosphere at home was unpredictable and often toxic. My worry and anxiety were genuine and very painful. Who was going to walk through the door that day? Good, sober Dad or Big John, the whiskey drinker? Over and over, I played out each possible scenario in my head. Of course, I could never accurately predict the outcome. Being preoccupied with the fear of dealing with a volatile drunk was emotionally tiring and stressful. I prepared myself for the anticipated battles as though it was happening in the here and now. That feeling of dread was with me almost every day of my life as a child and young adult. My childhood was turned upside down by the devastating effects of my Dad's alcoholism. The internalized stress triggered a state of hypervigilance of my surroundings, particularly people and their actions. I carried this with me everywhere I went and became judgmental.

Interestingly, my judgementalism became not only thoughts but feelings. My attempts at control were futile, but it never stopped me from trying. Control is a form of safety. I often felt something terrible would happen if I let go of a situation.

Even in the darkest moments in our home, the traumatic incidents between Mom and Dad always involved alcohol. Once again, it was the booze that was talking. I vividly recall the painful memories. I believe that my experiences and lessons learned are typical for a kid growing up in a dysfunctional home. In my case, our house was plagued with mixed messages, disappointments, and intense, terrifying emotions.

A Day in the Life

One of my most traumatic recollections of my father being in a volatile, drunken rage is also the most painful. I was in grammar school when, one evening, four of us children were sitting around the kitchen table trying to do our homework after dinner. Both of my parents had a drink in front of them. Mom had a glass of beer, and Dad had his usual glass of whiskey. They started to argue over something trivial when Mom called Dad an actor and told him to grow up. Specifically, she said, "You're an actor, just like John Barrymore." Man, did that trigger a reaction. As we braced for the fallout, my brothers and I put down our pencils and schoolbooks.

"John Barrymore?" Dad barked. "You say that again, and I'll spit in your face."

Not one to back down herself, Mom looked him in the eye and said again, "You're an actor, just like John Barrymore."

With that remark, he spits in her face in front of us kids.

Mom screamed in disbelief, "How could you do that?" "You miserable bastard!"

As we watched in shock, the yelling and screaming escalated. We scattered, leaving our homework strewn on the floor, and retreated to our bedrooms. We cried ourselves to sleep as the argument continued late into the night.

The next day, not a word was mentioned about the previous night. We got up and left for school as usual. I was shocked, embarrassed, and concerned for Mom as I headed out the door to school. As a kid, I knew that this incident was degrading. I would never spit on another person. However, I could not concentrate all day, dreading the sound of the bell signaling the time to go home.

Home? Home? To what? The lesson from this incident, like the others, was don't talk and don't feel.

I didn't realize it at that time, but as I grew older, there would be many more incidents of rage and violence fueled by alcohol. My ability to concentrate on schoolwork was hindered due to my tumultuous home environment. Perhaps this was the reason why I was held back in the second and fifth grades. My teachers were unaware of what was happening in my home or how to help me.

One evening, when I was about twelve years old, us kids were already asleep when we were abruptly awakened by shouting. My parents were drinking and arguing again, most likely over money, which was a recurring issue. The yelling and threats intensified to the extent that my mother had to call the police. The house was in an uproar, and the screaming did not cease.

I stood in the living room, tears streaming down my face, trembling with fear and pleading with my parents and the police to make it all stop. They did not respond, as if they couldn't see or hear me. The painful lump in my throat grew even tighter, making it difficult to swallow. It felt as though I was being choked. The pain was unbearable. More pain and trauma. *Why wasn't anyone stepping in to help? Why doesn't God respond to my desperate pleas?*

Finally, the policeman said, "John, why don't we go for a walk so your kids can go to bed? It's late."

Dad walked outside into the night, presumably to cool off.

The next day, when I woke up, I walked past my parent's bedroom, where they were still asleep. I went downstairs and waited, sitting alone, trying to process what had happened the night before. I heard my father getting up, and my heart started to race as the emotions from the previous night began to resurface. My father came down the stairs and said, "Good morning, Tim. I'm going to go across the street and pick up the paper. I'll be back in ten minutes." That was it. Not one word of explanation. No apology. Nothing. Processing of emotions does not happen in a house headed by an actively controlling alcoholic. Get over it, and don't feel it is how you survive.

I felt consumed by anger and an overwhelming feeling of loneliness. I had no one to talk to about the distressing events of the previous night. As a 12-year-old kid, I was left to grapple with my emotions in solitude. I handled this familiar home-grown trauma like I had countless times before by dissociating and internalizing everything, keeping my head down and mouth shut. I wish I were bold enough to run away. But I'm only a kid. Where would I go? Who could I trust? Who would offer support? I'm also afraid to return home some nights because of what could happen at home. I remain in constant vigilance for real or imaginary events. This continuous internal struggle of running away and the uncertainty of what could happen if I stayed was overwhelming. This is a common dilemma faced by innocent children who have experienced this trauma, knowing they cannot survive without the very parent who is causing this psychological harm.

I stayed because I had no choice. I stayed because I did not want to leave my Mom alone with this raging drunk. Somehow, I believed I had a duty to stay and protect her and my brothers. I stayed because I thought I could control his drinking. I continued yelling and arguing with my intoxicated Dad, believing I could change him. I never did change him, but it never stopped me from charging into the brawl. Unfortunately, this state of hypervigilance grew stronger each year and spilled into my dysfunctional decision-making process.

That incident was not the only time the police were called to our house in the middle of the night for a "domestic dispute." I lost count of these ugly, angry shouting matches. It would always occur after my parents had been drinking, often heavily. Arguments became louder and louder. Hurtful words were exchanged, and threats were made. There were crazy accusations about spending money, drinking too much, feeling ignored or disrespected. Each tells the other that they are drinking too much. Usually, there would be a shove or a slap. Mom hit Dad over the head with a dinner plate a couple of times.

My brothers and I would be upstairs in bed, trembling under the covers, crying, and hoping the shouting would subside. When the screaming was particularly bad, I would jump into the fray, screaming hurtful words and threatening Dad, trying my best to stop it. I do not remember Dad punching Mom, but he came very close, and the threat was always present and real. He did shove her, though. As I've mentioned, Dad was a large man with powerful, strong hands, and there's no doubt he would have caused significant injury. Someone might have stepped in to end the madness if physical injuries had been observed. I don't know. But I know that the constant drinking, threats, arguing, and the paralyzing tension in our home were much more harmful to me than any punch in the face.

Once, when Dad did push Mom, she fell against the iron radiator in the living room, resulting in a cut to her head. She was bleeding and screamed in pain. Everyone was yelling, crying, and pleading for Dad to stop. One of my brothers said, "Call the cops." It was the only source of help that we could think of. I knew the number well and remember it to this day. Every time the police entered our home, it was terrifying and shameful.

It's after one in the morning when two Boston police officers enter our tiny, crowded living room. Shortly after, a patrol sergeant and two more officers arrive, as Mom explains what happened. Dad is standing there, drunk, attempting to minimize the situation, telling the cops he is a Boston Firefighter. I yell for the cops to take my father out of the house. "I can't stand this," I plead as tears stream down my face, and I can hardly swallow because of the terror and anger. Mom also wanted Dad to leave. But Dad states loudly, "This is my house, and I'll do what I want."

Five police officers were surrounded by three or four crying kids, an assaulted wife, and a drunken, angry, and adamant Big John. I know these guys do not want to fight him. He is a large, intimidating man and would put up quite a battle. The sergeant in charge again says, "John, just take a walk around the block and cool off." That isn't good enough for me because of my fear that he will return and things will escalate. I plead for the cops to arrest him and get him out of the house. I recall asking myself, why am I in the middle of all of this?

No one responds. It is as though they don't see me. I'm shaking, and the painful knot in my throat only gets more intense. Attempting to swallow feels like I am being strangled. Why doesn't someone make this stop?

The sergeant says, "John, look what you're doing to these kids."

Before my father says anything, I yell, "He doesn't give a shit about us."

Dad is standing there with that stupid, vacant stare we all recognize. His eyes are bloodshot red and glassy, his forehead tense, his slurred speech, and his movements slow and awkward. He slowly and defiantly repeats, "This is my house," as he deliberately elongates the letter "s" in the word "house" for an excessive amount of time. The police officers can't tell if this is submissive or passive-aggressive. They stand there with bewildering faces, not knowing what is the next move.

It seems the madness continued forever, with us crying kids and Mom and Dad hurling insults and accusations at each other. Finally, the sergeant says, "John, why don't you go to the firehouse and sleep it off? I'll drive you there." Dad thinks it over for a second. He walks into the kitchen, grabs his keys, and says, "I'm going to the firehouse." Everyone stops and remains perfectly still, including the cops, and watches him walk out the back door.

Like many other events in the house, this was not discussed or acknowledged. The day after this incident, Dad walked back into our home, said hello—nothing more—and went upstairs to bed as if nothing had happened. When I discussed the situation with my Mother, she said she would talk to him and persuade him to stop drinking. Of course, this never happened. I pleaded with her to obtain a restraining order to remove him from the house. She said, "Where would he go? He'll end up homeless, living in the streets." She loved him and could look past his drunkenness, but I refused to do the same. I would have put him out of the house in a second to protect us if it had been up to me, but I was just a kid without a voice. I believe my Mom remained utterly unaware of the immense feelings of fear and sadness I experienced.

The only action I could take was to search the house for his bottles of alcohol and throw them out. It was not difficult to find his whiskey in our cramped house. He hid his alcohol in two places: under clothes in his bureau or in the closet. Each time I discovered his whiskey bottle, I would empty some of it into the toilet and watch it go down the drain, hoping that would end the pain and fear. It never worked. The bottle was always replaced with another one. My heart sank when I watched him bring the brown paper bag with the pint of whiskey into the house. The ubiquitous liquid poison that tormented innocent kids. It was a sign of trouble on the horizon.

I am certain that whenever there was an incident in our household, the neighbors must have heard the screaming and witnessed the police cars parked outside. Yet, they turned a blind eye to the destruction and trauma that unfolded in our home. It was a common belief in those days that it was not their concern. Neighbors assumed that the families would resolve things and thought it best not to intervene. It is ironic because I'm sure that if my Mom had witnessed or heard such turmoil occurring in someone else's home, she would courageously speak up and offer assistance, as she had done on several occasions. It is difficult when you are in the midst of chaos to find a solution because you lose hope, despair takes hold, and you believe that there is no way out. I felt trapped because I knew this situation would continue indefinitely, with no end in sight.

Months later, I sat in the living room watching TV on a Saturday afternoon as the arguing commenced. Mom and Dad were at the kitchen table, and Dad was loaded, and the whiskey was talking again. I had no idea what they were arguing about this time, and, once again, it escalated into a shouting match. I was crying, trembling, pleading with God to make it stop. *Why was God unresponsive to my prayers?* I went upstairs to my room to escape the battle. As I walked past my parent's bedroom, I noticed the crucifix on the wall. I stood before it, crying and pleading with God to make it stop. Nothing happened—nothing but silence from God. He is not a presence that will protect me. The only thing I heard was my parents screaming at each other. Once again, I wished I had the courage to run away, but I could not. I was frightened. I couldn't articulate what I was feeling. I grabbed the crucifix off the wall and threw it onto the floor. I was so angry and hurt that I did not care. I said to myself, "*I'm done with God!*"

Another Saturday afternoon, Dad tore the house apart in a drunken rage. He pulled every piece of clothing from every closet and emptied the contents of every dresser. He tipped over their bed, throwing the mattress across the room. Downstairs in the kitchen, pots and pans landed on the floor. He capped off this fury by slamming a heavy cast iron skillet against the porcelain sink. Big John wielded the skillet like a rolled-up newspaper used to swat a fly. The skillet broke into several pieces, and a large part of the sink broke off. He was screaming that he was sick and tired of this mess and wanted everything thrown out and cleaned up. His uncontrollable rage was terrifying to witness. My Mom, my two younger brothers, and I fled for our safety and to try to find my older brothers to warn them not to go home. Scared and embarrassed, I ran to the church rectory to ask our parish priest to come to our home and speak with Dad as soon as possible.

This was not the only time we fled in terror. When I was about eleven, late one night, my Mom gathered my two younger brothers and me, and we ran to our neighbors for safe shelter. This was my friend Mike's house on the same block as ours. Mike and I were the same age and often played together in the courtyard and his basement. I recall that night laying on the floor in Mike's house, listening to his Mom trying to console my Mom. This incident was embarrassing and confusing for me. Mom did not feel safe returning home until after the sun was up. I recall how my friend looked at me as my Mom tried to explain to his mother why we needed a safe place to stay until my Dad went to sleep. Mike was perplexed and frightened as my family brought our fear and insanity into his home.

Later, Mike's father returned from an all-night fishing trip. I vividly remember the shock and confusion on his face as my Mom explained what had happened. He could not believe what he was hearing and seeing that night.

After that night, I never set foot in my friend's house again. It was as though my friend had abandoned me. Did that family now fear the raging alcoholic in their neighborhood? This event changed the dynamics of a friendship, and it was never the same.

When these alcohol-induced arguments occurred in our home, I would listen to the discussion and become hypervigilant, focusing on the yelling, name-calling, and screaming as it escalated. Tension rising, fear growing, I wanted it to stop. It was not my fight, yet I was drawn into it and waited to see what unfolded. *How do I stop this chaotic and unpredictable insanity? Do I jump into the fight to protect Mom? Do I walk away?* I couldn't escape. The anxiety affected me physically and emotionally. The trauma remained, eating away at me, as I tried to continue my day as if nothing happened.

After these blowouts, I sometimes had brief conversations with one or both of my parents. They would tell me it would be okay, and Dad would stop drinking. My father knew he was drinking excessively and promised not to do it again. However, two weeks later, he would come home, with his breath reeking of whiskey. "He did it again," I would announce to Mom.

This pattern of disappointment repeated itself again and again. How often would I have my hopes up only to realize I had been lied to and disappointed again? This frustration built up. In another situation, maybe I could have ignored it, but how could I go on living under the same roof with my Dad, who continually tormented his family? How does a kid escape this? I paid the price typical for children of alcoholics by becoming codependent and losing my sense of self while experiencing anger, shame, and unbearable loneliness through no fault of my own.

By age fourteen, I realized I had to develop my own agency to survive. I had become a resilient, desensitized, controlling, independent, enabling, and people-pleasing young man. I am a codependent individual whose actions may have appeared noble on the surface, but internally, I lacked a sense of self and emotional awareness. This aspect of my identity revolved around my unhealthy relationship with my father. My codependent behavior was an attempt to protect myself and find peace. Instead, the gravitational forces of dysfunction were relentless and pulled me into the chaos of living with an active alcoholic. I was not my true self. Sadly, I lived in isolation and had no understanding of my own identity. My self-esteem was based on my experiences in my home and what I thought you would think about me if you discovered the truth. I survived by living in a dissociative state, allowing me not to feel the intense emotional pain. This was often the survival mode that I lived in because I was not strong enough to cope with constant feelings of fear, confusion, and abandonment. A child's home should be the safest place for them, but it's not when you live with an erratic, active alcoholic.

I was angry at every part of my father—the way he moved, the smell of his body, even that stupid grin on his face whenever he walked through the door. I failed to see the good and spiritual man others saw: the brave firefighter who attended Mass each week. I only saw a raging alcoholic and hypocrite. I grew to dislike him more. Dad was no longer my invincible hero but a deeply flawed man who was disappointing, unreliable, and often feared.

When Mom and Dad announced it was time for us to brush our teeth, say our prayers, and go to bed, dutifully, we always kissed our parents goodnight and marched upstairs. But now I had had enough of the charade. I was fearful of my father. At times, I loathed him. One night, at bedtime, I finally took a stand and said, "I'm too old for that. Kissing goodnight is for kids." I walked past Dad without remorse or regret. Out of the corner of my eye, I could see the surprise, dismay, and sadness on his face. I did not care. I had stood up for myself and never again kissed him goodnight, goodbye, or anything else.

Along with this act of revolt, I also stopped praying. In my mind, God had abandoned me. God had ignored my pleas for help. I believed God left me to deal with this alcohol-fueled insanity.

Fuck them was my attitude toward my Dad and God. I figured I was better off without them and refused to act as if everything was all right. The two beings—Dad and God—who were supposed to nurture and care for me had done the opposite.

Previously, I had prayed at dinner, in church, on family day trips when getting into the car, and each night when I went to bed. Prayer was not working and had not been for what seemed an exceptionally long time in my short life. That evening, I terminated my connection with God, determined to be self-reliant, without Dad or God.

This bold action was a pivotal moment in my life. I had no idea that the resentment I developed for my Dad and God would be so profound and deep in my inner spirituality. It would stay with me for decades. This resentment turned on me, made me angry, and almost killed me several times. It separated me from Dad and God. I nurtured and cultivated this resentment and held onto it because I knew I was right, and they had both wronged me. I was determined to run my own life but was clueless about the cost to my humanity and authentic self.

For me, inner spirituality and hope were missing. I did not possess peace of mind or the ability to access it. Mine was a shadow of an interior life. It did not register, nor was I aware I could find something to turn to in times of desperation. I was still a child at that point in my life, and God did not exist for me. Removing God from my life was an unfortunate mistake with severe consequences that I could not understand. I was alone and would figure it out (or so I thought) with determination and grit.

I set my goals to get an education and a decent career to move out of the project and free myself from living under the same roof with an abusive alcoholic.

I was fourteen when my parents decided we would take a family trip to Niagara Falls, the family's most extended trip ever. Maybe it was a reward for the challenging year our family had had. Mom was now battling cancer but felt well enough to travel. When Mom and Dad asked me if I was excited about the trip, I informed my parents, in a firm and confident voice, that I was not going and that they should go without me. They were incredulous. We argued for a few days, but I stood firm. Some of the arguments became heated and loud. I said I had no interest in going and would be fine and could take care of myself. The truth was that I had no desire to be around Dad when he was drinking. Being stuck in the car or a hotel room so far from home was a frightening proposition, and I wanted no part of it. Eventually, they capitulated and went on vacation with my two younger brothers without me.

When they returned, I was told the vacation was lovely and showed many scenic family Polaroid pictures of the trip. I would have enjoyed experiencing Niagara Falls, but I had asserted my independence to escape Dad's drinking. I gave up something special because of the fear inside me. I lost out because of someone else's drinking. It was a sad occasion thirty-five years later when I made a trip to Niagara Falls. I wondered how much I would have enjoyed being on that once-in-a-lifetime trip with my Mom and two younger brothers so many years ago.

A Worried Childhood

Compared to other kids in the neighborhood, I was generally a well-behaved "good kid." I did not act out or get into trouble, and the police never came to arrest me. Although I struggled academically in grammar school, my teachers didn't request parental meetings because of my behavior. I just wanted to be a normal kid with hopes and dreams, but I constantly felt ashamed and abandoned to my core. I was always overly critical of myself, relying on all-or-nothing thinking and self-doubt to guide my decisions. I would second-guess my choices and feel regret before knowing the outcome. I believed that asking for help would make me seem weak or stupid. These are common experiences for children of alcoholic parents.

Once a happy-go-lucky kid, I attempted to be invisible and stoic while suppressing my hopes and dreams. Becoming a chameleon would ensure that I would not be the scapegoat for the next drunken outburst. I believed I could shield myself from the unpredictable drunken father by concealing my anger, fear, and shame. I don't remember exactly when, but I became detached from my true feelings at a young age. It seemed necessary not to talk, trust, or feel if I wanted to survive, control the situation, and keep the peace. As a kid, I did not know how to articulate what was happening in my life, express my true feelings, or ask for help. I was a lost soul entering adulthood, feeling adrift and disconnected from my own identity.

Fear and worry enveloped me incessantly. While sitting in my classroom, I would find myself consumed by thoughts of what might be happening at home with my parents. I constantly thought about Dad's drunken tirades, dreading when it would happen again. The ability to be present at the moment and genuinely enjoy life's experiences felt like a luxury reserved for others and certainly not for me. At the same time, I was trapped in a cycle of fear and hypervigilance.

A friend asked me why I didn't confide in my teachers about my home life. The truth is, I didn't know how to express my feelings because we never discussed them. I also believe it is because I had bad experiences with teachers and feared them. By the time I reached middle school, I had learned which teachers to avoid when they were sometimes hungover and grouchy. I distinctly remember witnessing a distressing incident involving a sixth-grade student and our teacher. This student was grabbed by the arms, lifted off his feet, and thrown against a wall by the teacher. The teacher was a former college wrestling champ who argued with the kid sitting beside me. The grown man, well over six feet tall and muscular, told the kid to bring his father up to school, and he would deal with him too, "if his father has any balls."

Hearing this insult and challenge was devastating for him. It was difficult for the kid to listen to this from a teacher, particularly in front of his classmates. It was sad to witness a child's spirit shattered by these words. He had a meltdown, started crying and impulsively threw a wooden ruler at the teacher. That's when the teacher lunged, grabbed the kid, violently shook him, and slammed him into the blackboard.

He and I remained friends, but he never bounced back from that traumatic experience. Maybe he didn't have my resilience, or there was more trauma in his home. I will never know. Over the years, I watched him develop his drinking problems and struggle with life. Many of the kids in my middle school were also living with alcoholic parents, and we all had the same street smarts and character traits of a child of an alcoholic. I always wanted to speak with that bully teacher and congratulate him for emotionally destroying a sixth grader. Nice job, jackass!

The psychological fear I experienced induced a lifetime of physical manifestations such as stomachaches, headaches, and other discomforts. My mother took me to the doctor several times to determine the source of my stomach pains and cramps. On one visit, the doctor asked my Mom if I was under any pressure. Mom replied, "He's only twelve years old. He's not under pressure!"

Along with the stomach ailments, I had other difficulties that affected my performance in school and work, including the inability to concentrate, hypervigilance, sensitivity, and social anxiety. The only consistent thing was my inability to relax and my heightened fear of failure. I worried I would be stuck in this dysfunctional merry-go-round of insanity for my entire life if I lost control.

My teenage years were full of overwhelming emotional and physical anguish. I found it challenging to be optimistic, have hope, and envision opportunities beyond my current circumstances. I felt trapped in an unhealthy and sorrowful environment, desperately seeking an elusive escape. Breaking free from this situation seemed futile because I believed the world outside my home and neighborhood mirrored the same unpredictable bleakness. I would only be going from bad to worse, and my efforts to control an uncontrollable current situation seemed manageable. At least I knew who the participants were in my house. I mistakenly assumed that the dysfunction within our household was a reflection of the world at large. The outside world appeared vast, dangerous, and unpredictable for this kid. It's better to remain in the muck and mire I'm familiar with than to venture out. These were the defining experiences of my formative years.

Eventually, I internalized this dysfunction, lost confidence, and started not liking myself. *Am I weak and broken? Is all this my fault? Why can't I just roll with all this chaos like everyone else seems to be doing? Is something wrong with me? Am I being punished? What the fuck is going on?*

My poverty of words and fear of healthy risk-taking prevented me from articulating my problems or making the necessary changes to improve my situation. Seeking help involved risk-taking, and the potential for emotional pain (shame) was too high. All I had were my survival instincts, clinging to resilience and perseverance. Let me tell you that on some days, I felt like I was barely hanging on by a thread. Adding to my inner turmoil were the comments I often heard about how my Dad was such a great guy. My tormentor was on a pedestal, respected by the entire community. All I could do was smile and say, he is, and Thanks, when I thought and experienced the opposite. My life was a mess and a tale of the absurd.

I never considered it a problem that Mom had a beer after dinner. I never witnessed her slurring her words, stumbling, and falling. She never appeared hungover in the morning or stayed in bed all day. She had a slight buzz after a wedding or special occasion but did not seem impaired. She never drove the family car while under the influence of alcohol. Our conversation regarding alcohol was always about Dad's drinking and behavior. She was always afraid he would end up on Dover Street in Boston's South End, a notorious area for drunks, prostitutes, and flophouses.

Mom was the rock in our family, the person you could count on to fix any problem, from finding lost items to dressing bleeding wounds. She was always there for us. Whenever one of us kids couldn't find something, such as a sock or hockey stick, she would recite a simple prayer to St. Anthony. "Dear St. Anthony, please come around. Something is lost and must be found." This prayer assured us that St. Anthony was working on our behalf and that whatever we sought would reappear. She prayed often and kept a set of rosary beads beside her bed. I would see her in bed praying with the rosary beads early in the morning. Perhaps she was praying that Dad would control his drinking?

How my mother could forgive my father and shake it off has always baffled me. Looking back, I can now see that she did not fully understand the implications of enabling an active alcoholic who many times terrorized our family.

Living like this wreaked havoc on my life and our family. Imagine sitting in your living room, and a hurricane strikes without warning. That was what it was like, and I did not understand how to handle the trauma.

Mom's Illness

When I was fifteen, my mother's cancer returned, and she started to become seriously ill. She experienced excruciatingly painful medical conditions for the next three years. She had a hysterectomy and was diagnosed with colon and lung cancer. She rarely complained and never displayed any self-pity. My two oldest brothers had moved out and gotten on with their lives by then. My father was still drinking, working, and doing what he could to help raise the four of us living at home. I was no longer just helping Mom in the kitchen but taking over more responsibility for preparing meals for everyone.

I only recall discussing my mother's condition when my older brother and I returned from a hospital visit. Mom had had surgery to assess the severity of her lung cancer and to remove a tumor. She looked so uncomfortable, lying in the hospital bed with several tubes on her side. I talked to her and held her hand, trying my best to reassure her that she would be all right even though I felt despondent.

On the ride home, my brother said, "Things don't look good. She's probably going to die."

"I know," I said. I fully understood what was happening and what it meant. I felt sad and helpless. I did not want to lose my Mom. She had always been so good to all of us, and despite her unwillingness to remove Dad from the house, I always felt she had good intentions and was doing her best. I also thought we shared a special connection because we were concerned about my father's drinking. I spoke to no one about processing how I felt about her illness.

I was eighteen when Mom was home, primarily bedridden and dying from cancer. Because of colon cancer, she had to use a colostomy bag. Cleaning and changing her bags were difficult. The smell of human waste, added to the smell of cigarettes, created a foul stench we learned to tolerate.

To my father's credit, he tried his best to hold it together. We all did. But one night, he snapped. No longer could he come home from work and lay in the same bed with a woman who was thin as a rail and slowly and painfully dying of cancer. Late one evening, he lost his ability to tolerate the odor of death. They were both in bed when I heard an argument ensuing. And then I heard a loud thump. I ran to their room, and Dad was helping Mom up from the floor. The mattress had been turned over and was partially on the floor. I asked what had happened.

"Mom fell trying to get into the bathroom," Dad said.

Worried, I helped Mom into the bathroom and asked her if she was alright. She assured me she was, and we all went back to bed.

After my father left for the firehouse the following day, I asked my mother what had happened.

She looked at me and said, "He told me I smelled like crap. Then he pushed the mattress over, and I rolled out of bed onto the floor."

I was enraged. I did my best to help Mom return to bed, getting her as comfortable as possible. It was a sweltering day; the only relief was from a window fan. I waited for my father to return from the firehouse that evening.

He walks in, wearing the shit-eating grin that only a drunk can wear. Once again, the smell of cheap whiskey permeates his skin. I was not too fond of his appearance. His forehead is tense and tightened back, and he has that *I'm-drunk-again* face. Of course, I know the answer, but I boldly challenge him, "Have you been drinking again?"

He does not look at me or answer. I jump up and step toward him. "You're fucking drunk again. You shoved my mother, who is in pain and dying of cancer, out of her bed last night. You're a piece of shit! I'm sick of you! Let me tell you something. If you ever do anything like that again, I will put a bullet in your fucking head. I will shoot you in your head!"

I continue yelling, "You're not a man! You're a drunken coward! You should get the fuck out of this house and leave us all alone!"

He looks down and starts to shed tears, which does not slow down my tirade.

"I will fucking kill you, and you know I have the gun to do it. You assaulted and hurt your wife, my mother! I'm not going to let that happen again! And if I can't get my gun, I'll stick a knife in your heart while you are passed out. No one will give a shit."

He stood there, not saying a word. Words cannot undo the brutality of his actions.

I tell him, "I'm going out now. Why don't you return to the firehouse and sleep it off?"

I stood up to Big John. I hated him, not only for what he had done to my mother but also for what was happening to me. I was taking on his rage, which was becoming part of me. By internalizing the trauma and shame along with other dysfunctional character traits, it had become my identity. This is not my true self but someone I believe I am. I was consumed by fear, resentment, insecurity, and a profound sense of brokenness. I hated being trapped by these feelings. Nobody should have to live like this, particularly a teenager. Because of these continuing barrages of terrible experiences, I developed an ability to stand up to authority. I was not afraid of him and committed to carrying out every word I said. When a child can stand up to the supposedly most authoritative person in their life, no one will get in their way when they feel they are right and need to speak the truth.

An Insider View of My Dad's Firehouse.

In attempting to understand the challenges I experienced because of my Dad's alcohol abuse, I realized it would be helpful to speak with members of the Boston Fire Department (BFD) who both knew my Dad and spent some time in the same firehouse. Most of Dad's World War II contemporaries have passed on or are unavailable. I wanted to locate people who would speak the truth and understand my intentions while not being overly concerned with protecting the reputation of the Fire Department.

Fortunately, I found several men who started working as Boston firefighters in the 1970s and 1980s and spent their entire careers as firefighters. Two of these men were from the same neighborhood in South Boston and knew several members of my family. Another rewarding aspect of interviewing these men was that they had long-term sobriety. As sober individuals, they offer an interesting perspective. These men told me it was difficult to be sober when alcohol use and abuse was rampant in many BFD stations. I was grateful that they agreed to speak with me.

They explained that many firehouses had the reputation of being a place where men drank on duty. They said, "You quickly learned the firehouses where some men worked hard and at other firehouses where men drank hard. Some guys were attracted to that lifestyle." The house supervisors often drank and looked the other way when things got out of hand. It's challenging and conflicting to reprimand a guy for drinking on duty when you occasionally drink with him in the same firehouse. Some people would transfer to a firehouse because they knew they could drink without consequences. Men with drinking problems often would be assigned to another firehouse where drinking on duty was accepted. Others would request a transfer so that they could drink and not be disturbed by a supervisor. The bottom line is that many supervisors were not doing their job, and the culture of alcohol use and abuse was widespread.

I asked specifically about my Dad's house in the South End of Boston and the amount of drinking in that firehouse. One man recalled, "They had a bar in the basement." It was like a clubhouse with tables and chairs set up with bottles of alcohol kept in lockers for the men to consume. When the alarm bell rang to respond to a fire, the men would run to the trucks, and off they would go to battle a fire or assist someone. It was common for some men to be intoxicated when answering a call and running up a ladder into a burning building. My Dad's firehouse was one of the busiest in the city during this time there. Many believed they were entitled to a drink after battling a fire. "Everyone does it, so it must be all right," one man said. They recalled how difficult staying sober was for anyone working in this environment.

I asked why and how this was allowed to happen. I was told these men were a "brotherhood" who depended on each other for their safety and "cover." They all looked the other way at one time or another, compromising their ability to speak up. It is challenging to turn someone in when you work, sleep under the same roof, share stories about your kids, and eat meals with that person. They worked and drank hard and covered for one another, which was expected and acceptable.

They added that these guys went to the firehouse to live when they were asked to leave their homes. This gave them an understanding shoulder to cry on when the "mean wife asks me to leave for no reason!" Some guys would sleep and drink in the house for weeks until they could return home. With that much time on your hands and in a comfortable haven, it was the perfect place to drink and feel bad for yourself. One added, "You must appreciate the situation, Tim. Your dad was a good firefighter, a well-respected man. Everyone knew Big John as a good guy, working two jobs to raise six kids in the projects. You don't turn him in and jeopardize his paycheck. That would hurt his family." So, they enabled him, I asked. He shrugged and said, "What can I say?" "Today, we know that is not how to help a person struggling with substance abuse, but back then, things were different," he said.

Disputes in the firehouse were handled in-house by the individuals involved. Arguments and fistfights occurred, but they learned to get along like any family living under the same roof. You might have a dispute with a colleague one day and need them to watch your back the next day. Things were resolved by returning to the back of the firehouse and working it out. The next day, they would sit at the dining table talking about the Red Sox baseball game as though nothing had happened.

One firefighter told me of an incident while responding to an automobile accident. When the police officer came to question the driver, he asked, "Have you been drinking?" The driver, laying on the ground, having a neck braced applied by a firefighter, stated emphatically no. The Officer says, "You're lying." "I can smell it!" He was smelling the breath of the first responder applying the neck brace.

They also told me about one guy who was reprimanded for drinking continuously for days while on the job. He was prepared to meet with the Captain to discuss why he missed a shift at the station. The discussion hadn't even started when he shouted his defense, saying he had been working at another job, lost track of time, and would never miss a shift again. The captain looked at him in disbelief because this guy had been in the firehouse in a blackout for two days and had missed all the fire alarms. The consequence was to order him to "sleep it off and never do that again."

I asked if there were any firehouses in the city where alcohol was not allowed while on duty. They said there were many houses where the supervisors did their jobs, and alcohol use was not tolerated. It was unacceptable; if you didn't like it, you asked for a transfer. One man recalled the time when a new Captain was assigned to a firehouse where there was a vending machine that dispensed cans of beer. When the Captain noticed it, he asked what was in that vending machine. One firefighter told him it was a Coca-Cola machine. The captain informed the men he wanted it out of the firehouse that day. When the men balked, he picked up an axe and destroyed the vending machine. When one guy attempted to intervene, the Captain threatened to hit him in the head with the axe. End of discussion. Those guys were upset and indignant that someone would remove their beer dispenser. They said an arrogant sense of entitlement was common among the men who drank during work. Over the years, many alcoholics I have known have this same sense of entitlement regarding alcohol.

We talked about how things are today versus the 1970s and 1980s. They were confident that the response to drinking on the job is entirely different today. People would be fired from their jobs if they drank and abused alcohol as they did back in the day. But first, they would be offered employee assistance services and an opportunity to get help for alcohol dependency. It should not have been acceptable back then, and unfortunately, it was.

One of these men stated that every other household in your neighborhood (housing project) seemed to have a drunken mom or dad. The kids never spoke about it but tolerated the situation as best they could. Kids don't have many options. He recalled his shame when he and his friends saw one of their parents stumble home intoxicated. "The only thing we could do was joke about it and be thankful that it wasn't my dad walking past the kids on the corner."

People back then were learning that alcoholism was a disease. It wasn't until 1956 that the American Medical Society declared alcoholism a medical condition, not a moral issue. It took many years for people to understand and accept this. These men returned from the war and started drinking and working as though excessive drinking was normal behavior before this disease declaration. Public drinking was just considered a low-level moral crime. This was new territory, and they did not understand the long-term impact on the families.

My Dad and his fellow fighters were approximately thirty-eight years old in 1956. By then, he and my Mom had five kids and one more on the way and had experienced two stillbirths and one miscarriage. They persevered because they thought their lives would be rich and blessed. After all, they considered children to be gifts from God. Dad and his friends had been drinking ever since the war and had probably developed a tolerance for alcohol. Couple that with the culture that normalized drinking, and as my friend said, "They went too far down the rabbit hole."

They would see someone as a good person, and intervention would only destroy their lives and family's lives. You didn't want to see anyone get arrested and lose a job, so you would pray that everything would be okay because "they're good guys." The Vendome Hotel tragedy of 1972 added to this. My friend said the tragedy further united the men, solidified their brotherhood, and saddened the Boston Fire Department. Unfortunately, this kind of rationalization and way of thinking occasionally continues today. As I write this memoir, it was reported this week in our local newspaper that a firefighter pleaded guilty to distributing highly addictive, dangerous drugs to other firefighters for the past four years. The story ended with the statement that the Fire Chief had "no comment." Does anyone have the courage not to look the other way but insist on treatment for these firefighters and their families? I believe there are many opportunities to change the culture and help someone trapped in addiction by not preserving the status quo.

Recognizing the impact of alcoholism on the productivity and safety of its members and their families, the National Fire Protection Association mandates that every Fire Department establish an assistance program for its members. These programs provide health and wellness education and professional counseling services such as substance use disorder treatment programs, suicide prevention, and PTSD. Many types of counseling services are available to firefighters for various issues, including critical incident debriefing, stress, and anxiety, using evidence-based treatment modalities that didn't exist when my Dad was a firefighter. Finding any treatment or support programs for the families of first responders was challenging.

The Toll Alcohol Takes on Children

In every conceivable manner, the family is a link
to our past, bridge to our future.
-Alex Haley

The research on adverse childhood trauma is both extensive and astonishing. Children raised in alcoholic families or where a parent has mental health issues start life with a disadvantage, unlike kids raised in emotionally healthy families.

Children raised in healthy, functioning homes by sober, loving parents experience a childhood totally opposite of a child raised in an alcoholic home. Functioning, healthy families don't live in constant fear. Open, healthy communication is encouraged and practiced within the family. Children can depend on their parents to meet their physical and emotional needs. Healthy families are taught to recognize and be sensitive to feelings, wants, and needs. Creativity, intimacy, and imagination are modeled, nurtured, and encouraged in healthy homes as the child becomes autonomous and independent. There may be beneficial alliances between siblings instead of becoming independent of one another because of the fear and shame permeating the home. Children are supported as they experience roles and develop personalities, preparing them to experience life beyond the family.

Many children raised in alcoholic homes experience PTSD and take on roles of surviving, keeping the peace, attempting to get their parents sober, and often becoming co-dependent. The alcoholic parent cannot meet their emotional needs, let alone his children's. Meeting their parent's needs becomes the primary function of the entire household. Critical developmental years are focused on safety, stabilizing the family, and the hopeless task of getting the family drunk sober. Which often leads to unhealthy co-dependency and other compulsive personalities by the victims. Co-dependency for me was to be absorbed in solving other people's problems while neglecting my own needs. I couldn't fix my problems, but I would charge in and fix yours. Today, I know that trying to get another person sober is impossible and wastes time and effort.

Children who were raised in alcoholic households often exhibit common character traits as a result of growing up in this dysfunctional environment, leading to the development of unhealthy compulsions. These compulsive behaviors can manifest in various forms, such as eating disorders, sex addictions, workaholism, gambling addictions, internet addictions, harmful thrill-seeking tendencies, perfectionism, impulse control issues, and, more commonly, alcoholism. An individual can experience one or more of these compulsions. During my teenage years, I firmly believed that I would never become an alcoholic or a workaholic. I had a firm resolve and confidence in my independence, assuring myself that such outcomes were not in store for this kid. I often told myself, "Just watch me; I'll never become an alcoholic."

These children struggle with creativity, imagination, trust, and intimacy. Their childhood roles are repressed while they take on the role of peacemaker, disciplinarian, child-adult, acting out child, scapegoat, or mascot of the family whose role is to entertain and deflect the pain and shame the family is experiencing at an enormous expense to themselves. I took on several of these roles during my formative years and carried them into adulthood. As with many children of alcoholics or trauma, these became my survival tools. We falsely believe we need these characteristics to survive the moment because we often lack proper skills. For many children of alcoholics, no one was available to model appropriate behavior to teach us otherwise. Instead, we act as the parent or savior of the family. Co-dependency is emotionally draining and conflicting, taking a tremendous toll on the survivor. It seemed I was always in conflict with my sense of true self.

Because of the environment that I was living in, I was rapidly becoming as emotionally sick as my Dad. The shame and traumas of abuse I experienced paralyzed me and remained with me into adulthood, blocking me from being vulnerable. Without being vulnerable, I could not grow or change. Without taking a risk, letting my guard down, allowing people to know me, or being part of something, I could not experience new things, mature as a healthy adult, or experience new relationships. I was stuck in a monotonous pattern where I felt safer living in the fallout from all the dysfunction than taking risks to improve my situation. I believed that if things were this bad in my home, it would be much worse in the outside world.

I survived by dissociation and compartmentalizing my emotions into internal silos, closets, or a filing cabinet in my head where I could place these emotions in a drawer and close it shut, giving me the feeling that I could control whatever happened or was about to happen each day. This unconscious defense mechanism allowed me to separate and stuff conflicting emotions deep within myself. This denial prevented me from acknowledging the emotional pain in my life. This strategy, or defense mechanism, was cumulative and would build up in my subconscious. Eventually, I needed an outlet to reduce the pressure.

I thought I was coping with life's challenges and getting through another day, but I always felt like I was juggling too many balls at once, never sure if one would drop. You could not tell by looking at me because, like most victims, I maintained a front, a false self, and hid it well. I lived this way as best I could. No child should have to experience anything like this. This is not healthy childhood development, and, for many, this adversity negatively influences and distorts their view of the world. I often sulked like a spoiled child, shutting down my emotions and appearing indifferent. I held back comments and avoided participating in conversations for fear of sounding inferior. I was flying under the radar so I would not be seen or heard. I acted in ways that were not my true self, which sometimes came off as being aloof. I used the sarcasm and judgementalism I learned as a kid so that you wouldn't interact with me and I would feel better when I put you down. I was always on the move, engaging in activities or work to escape internal and external conflicts that now controlled me.

The most discouraging fact of living this way was that small victories felt hollow, and I could not enjoy my accomplishments. Achievements brought attention to me, while my goal was to avoid attention because that could lead to anger or shame. I did not enjoy or experience the emotional rewards of success because I had no idea if I was successful because of my natural abilities or the unhealthy ones I had to develop to cope as a kid. As I began transitioning into adulthood, I had many fears and insecurities. I lacked a positive role model, which stunted my emotional development.

Alcohol became the outlet that relieved all these pressures and brought much-needed respite. Alcohol did the trick! After many years, I discovered that my codependency behaviors mistakenly worked until they didn't.

Getting Started

As I said earlier, most youngsters in my neighborhood started to drink as kids, but I started drinking at a very young age by having sips of beer as a child. I was very fond of beer, which was often on my mind when I was around adults. I would rub up against them like a puppy while asking for a "little sip" of their beer. This was before many of my friends in the project started to drink. Although I witnessed what alcohol did to my Dad, I knew at a young age I would be different. What happened to him will never happen to me!

Wherever there was an open beer, I would swoop in like a hungry seagull on a french fry. I enjoyed the taste of beer, and I loved the bubbles. I would ask for a sip from my parents, aunts, uncles, and any guests in our house. Whenever Mom's beer ran low, I volunteered to get her a refill. Dad usually drank whiskey, but he was not as generous as Mom and wasn't good for a sip when he had an occasional beer. When guests would get up to go to the bathroom, I would offer to mind their seats and help myself to their beer. I enjoyed the taste, effects, and feelings associated with alcohol.

One evening, when my father was working the night shift in the firehouse, Mom enjoyed a beer as we watched television. But I wasn't at all interested in the program that was on. I was obsessing over my Mom's beer, laser-focused on the bottle on the coffee table. As Mom reached the bottom of the bottle, I waited for the right moment to spring into action. I entered the kitchen, opened the fridge, grabbed a beer bottle, and opened it with a "church key," our term for a bottle opener. I took a big gulp as I came back into the living room.

Mom yelled out, "What are you doing? Did you open a beer?"

I quickly swallowed more, saying, "I'm getting it for you."

"I don't want a beer. It's time for bed."

That didn't stop me. I continued to gulp the beer until Mom jumped out of her chair and attempted to grab the bottle. She had one hand on my forehead and the other on the bottle, yelling, "Let go of that beer."

I took another mouthful as she tried to pull the bottle away and hold my head so she wouldn't crack the bottle on my teeth.

She finally said the magic words, "I'll tell your father if you don't let go of this bottle."

I consumed half a bottle and let out one loud belch as I walked upstairs to bed. Mom looked at me in disbelief. I was only ten years old and a delighted kid that night. I hoped we could do this again sometime soon.

Drinking with my friends started when we were about thirteen. Our supply mostly came from whoever had stolen alcohol from their parents. When that supply wasn't available, we would pool our cash and ask a local "wino" to "make the run" and purchase the alcohol. Getting someone to buy alcohol was always a challenge. *Who could we get to "make the run?"* Sometimes, we had to barter with a stranger and promise to give them a couple of our beers if they bought for us. No matter; we got the booze! As we got older, we learned which liquor stores did not ask for identification. It was all a joke.

Drinking beer as a teen meant getting a GIQ (giant imperial quart) of beer. Otherwise, we would split a six-pack. Sometimes, it was a bottle of Boone's Farm wine, which was nice and sweet. We drank vodka, blackberry brandy, rum, and ginger-flavored brandy during colder months. Pretty much anything we could get our hands on. My best friends were drinkers and stoners. I started smoking pot when I was fifteen. I didn't smoke much and limited it to mostly weekends. Weed was becoming increasingly available as hippies opposed to the Vietnam War all seemed to have weed for sale. This counterculture revolution celebrated sex, drugs, and rock 'n roll. If you smoked weed, then you were considered hip.

My parents were unaware of my marijuana use, and I never got caught. Coming home after smoking a joint, I'd walk into the house and announce that I didn't feel well and was going to bed. In my room, I had a cheap FM radio, posters of rock 'n roll bands, black lights, and a flashing string of Christmas lights. I'd switch on the black lights, gaze at the multi-color glow of the posters on the wall, put on some music, and drift off to sleep. I had discovered my escape from all the insanity.

I asked my buddy Brian to tell me where he was buying the weed. After we smoked a couple of joints, he confessed it was from his cousin, who was a dealer. He told me he helped his cousin break up the kilos into ounces. This was cool and exciting—something I'd seen only in movies or cop shows. He added that his cousin gave him free weed to help him. I couldn't believe it and wanted in on this deal. My heart was pumping with excitement as I enjoyed the thrill of this opportunity.

The following week, I was invited to go with Brian to his cousin's house. Our job was to break up a kilo of marijuana into ounces and help sell it. We would share an ounce of weed for doing this work—*plus whatever we could steal,* which we did!

The cousin's cockroach-infested apartment had walls that were painted black, and the windows were covered with cardboard and dark shades. There were mice droppings everywhere. Black lights and multi-colored Christmas lights flashed in the room. Posters on the walls gleamed in the black light. There was a stereo with two giant speakers in the room's corners. In the center of the room was a large, round, damaged wooden table. Previously, the electrical company used this wooden spool to hold the heavy copper cable. It was on its side in the middle of the living room, covered with burn marks and wine and beer stains. I felt like I had arrived.

The cousin dumped a pillowcase containing a kilo of weed onto the table as he told us, "it is from Mexico." Some weed had exotic names, but as long as someone declared it was "good shit" and not "ragweed," we would smoke it! Our only job was to break it up into "four-finger" ounces and put it into a plastic bag. "Don't overload the bag with twigs or seeds," he said.

"No problem," I said as if I were a seasoned pro. "I've done this before."

My buddy Brian and I assembled "four-finger" ounces until the cousin left the apartment to get some beers. He warned us not to smoke anything until he returned. We told him we would not, but as soon as he exited the door, we immediately lit up a joint to sample the goods. The next step was to take our cut—half an ounce each, which we put into bags and stuffed into our underwear. We felt like it was his fault for trusting two fifteen-year-old project kids.

We continued to work breaking the kilo into one-ounce bags, trying to look efficient for when he returned. He returned with some beers, looked over what we'd done, and gave us one ounce of marijuana for our work. We then sat around drinking beer and smoking joints. We helped this guy several times over the next year until he got busted, and our free weed ended abruptly. By then, I was a pro at rolling joints and smoking weed and could roll a joint with one hand.

When I was seventeen, my older brother took me to a bar for my first drink, which was thrilling. Being underage and naïve, I felt cool hanging with the older guys who were also underage. We entered this Irish bar in South Boston, and the five of us sat at a table, trying to look older. The bartender walked over, asking, "What are you having?" Each ordered a beer, but when the bartender asked me, I decided to be sophisticated and requested a "Sloe Gin, please." I had never had this, but I had overheard an adult order it once. It sounded like something an adult of legal age would request. The entire room seemed to stop and stare at me as the bartender looked at me incredulously and then turned to my brother. My brother told him to get me an effing beer. Then he turned to me and said, "If you ever do that again, I will effing kill you!" I almost blew it for everyone. The guys would have been pissed at me if they were kicked out of that bar for underage drinking!

Throughout high school, weed, hash, and alcohol became my escape. I drank and smoked every weekend. Summer was the best time to hang out with the guys and girls in the project. Drinking and smoking cigarettes and weed became the norm. It seemed like everyone was doing it, and it was a blast. We all used alcohol to socialize and, in some ways, to self-medicate. Alcohol removed my fears and insecurities; if I could have drunk every day back then, I would have.

My tolerance was growing along with my increased fondness for drinking and smoking weed. That year, the drinking age was lowered to eighteen. When I turned nineteen, I began the job

Whitey Bulger helped me get, working at the nightclub in Boston. *This is my scene*, I thought. *I'm a man. I've arrived!* Although, of course, I had pledged to myself never to emulate my father's behavior. I convinced myself that *I was going to be different. I could manage it. It wouldn't happen to me. It will never happen to me. Never.*

During the next few years, my alcohol consumption escalated. I was drinking and partying nearly every weekend. Hanging on the corner with my friends down "the square" in the project and smoking marijuana felt right. We savored the joking and teasing of each other and told funny stories. I felt accepted and part of something special when being with my friends.

I used alcohol to carry me through the day and, sometimes, the moment. Alcohol medicated my emotions, falsely elevated my self-worth, and removed the discomfort of being me. During these critical years, I continued to drink without understanding who I was or how I felt. Sometimes, I just wanted to get through the day without feeling used, abused, judged, or shamed.

Working and Drinking

In 1971, when I was seventeen, I was hired as a lifeguard for a state beach. I hoped to be assigned to Carson Beach because it was just a short walk from the project. I had frequented that beach as a kid, and my mother had taught me to swim there. My assignment was Nantasket Beach in Hull, Massachusetts, twenty-five miles from the project, with no direct route or convenient public transportation, as I tried to explain.

"That's your assignment," I was told. "Take the job or leave it. It's up to you."

I was determined to be independent and needed the money to "party," so I accepted the job without knowing how to get there and back home. I was also a young, budding workaholic, and nothing would stop me from getting my fix. My parents suggested I wait for something else to come along. Maybe something else would have turned up, but I could not wait. I was taking the job and would figure out how to get to work. Our family car was out of the question because Dad used it to get back and forth to his two jobs. Without another option, I decided to hitchhike the twenty-five miles from South Boston to Hull every day. I hoped to meet someone at work, maybe one of the other lifeguards, one who lived nearby and would give me a ride. As it turned out, all the other lifeguards were from the South Shore area, so I was on my own.

The crew I worked with were mostly college guys, and although I was still in high school, we did have a lot in common—we all liked to party, many of us smoked weed, and there was a party every weekend. Even though I was underage, I was drinking with college guys because of my size and ability to talk. I came to work numerous times hungover that summer. One of my buddies informed me that inhaling oxygen would lessen the effects of the hangover. There was a first aid room with an oxygen tank that was supposed to be used only in emergencies. I tried it many times, and it didn't help alleviate the pain of a hangover. The manager had to replace the tank more than usual that summer.

Occasionally, co-workers came to me looking to buy weed, which I was gladly able to provide. That was a wild summer. Many people who picked me up hitchhiking offered me a joint or a beer during the ride home. Alcohol and weed seemed readily available that summer. I lost count of how often I rode home in a car driven by a stranger, buzzed from weed or beer or both.

Each workday, I'd put on my orange lifeguard shirt, bathing suit, and bright orange pith helmet with the letters MDC Lifeguard. This made it much easier to get a ride. It was a bold decision to accept that job at my age without a car, but much more was happening in my life. I was branching out on my own and taking risks. I was seeking freedom, independence, and control of my life. Working was how I thought I could accomplish autonomy. I would have taken that job if it had been forty miles away. I thought work would somehow fix me and allow me to control all aspects of my life. I always had a job or two to earn money, which I equated with independence and control.

I was excited to show my mom when I received my first paycheck. Mom was in the kitchen preparing dinner when I told her how much I had made. She congratulated me and informed me about "room and board," explaining that everyone who worked in this house contributed some money each week. My older brothers contributed twenty dollars a week, and I was expected to do the same. I protested that this was *my* money. She agreed that it was my money and that my contribution would be helpful to our family budget. I informed her I didn't want to pay for room and board and that I should have my own bedroom for twenty dollars a week! Her reply was, "Then you should get your own apartment!" That made me stop for a moment and consider my options. I agreed to pay for room and board, but I should get the end piece of roast beef at Sunday dinner. She smiled at me as I handed over a new twenty-dollar bill. "We'll see," she said.

I enjoyed being a lifeguard at Nantasket Beach because of the responsibility, camaraderie, and weekly paycheck. One day, I was running late to work, and one of my older brothers let me borrow his car for the day. It was a nice change from hitchhiking. I parked his car at the police station directly across the street from the bathhouse because state employees were allowed to park there for free. A couple of hours into my shift, I was told to immediately report to the office in the bathhouse because the manager needed to speak to me. I thought *this couldn't be good*. I ran to the office. The manager told me to call home "now" because my brother wanted to speak with me. I thought, *This definitely must be bad news*.

I called the house, and my brother answered. "Thank God you called," he said. "Listen to me. Please do not open the glove compartment of my car. I have some stuff in there, and I do not want you or anyone else to go near it."

"What is it?"

"Never mind," he said. "Do not open the glove compartment, or you will never use my car again."

"Okay," I assured him. I told him his car was safely parked in the police parking lot, where nobody would touch it. I hung up and immediately went to the car to check the glove compartment. I mean, what did he think I was going to do? I had left all the windows open because of the summer heat, figuring no one would try to steal a car from a police parking lot.

When I opened the glove compartment, out rolled a bag of weed. It was less than an ounce, but I thought, *wow, this is wicked good!* I hit the jackpot and immediately took my cut. I reasoned that I was transporting his weed and taking the risk. If the police had stopped me, I was the one who would have been arrested. I had put my job at risk when I parked the car in a police parking lot with the windows open. My brother had no idea I had been smoking marijuana for two years. *When it comes to weed, he's a lightweight compared to me,* I thought.

I took enough weed to roll a couple of joints, returned to the beach, and enjoyed the remainder of my shift, mesmerized by the sparkling waves lapping against the shoreline. Nobody drowned. What a beautiful day!

When I arrived home, I handed my brother the car keys. I informed him that I had not opened the glove compartment, but I wanted assurance that whatever was there would not get him or anyone else in trouble. He brushed me off as I expected. But now that I knew where he kept his stash, I planned to visit whenever I needed a joint.

The following summer, I was transferred to a beach in South Boston. There was no more hitchhiking back and forth to work to the Town of Hull. I could walk to work and party more frequently with my friends. The crew I worked with were primarily local guys from Southie and Dorchester who partied and drank just like me. Looking back, I am not proud of my lifestyle, which continued for the next twenty years. It continued even as I promised myself I would not drink like my father. *Never,* I told myself. Even though I made poor decisions repeatedly, I thought I was better. I was confident I would recognize and stop drinking before it became a problem. I was also entering my senior year of high school.

1972

The Vendome luxury hotel was built in 1871 in Boston's Back Bay, just north of Copley Square. At that time, this gorgeous building captured the city's brightest hopes. My parents celebrated their wedding reception there on February 25, 1942. We were reminded of this whenever our family drove down Commonwealth Ave and passed the building or when we watched the short film of their wedding and reception in the Vendome ballroom.

On the afternoon of Father's Day, Saturday, June 17, 1972, the Vendome Hotel was largely empty except for a few workers performing renovations. One of the employees discovered that a fire had begun in an enclosed space between the third and fourth floors. A working fire was reported to the fire department at 2:44 p.m. Subsequent alarms were rung at 2:46, 3:02, and 3:06. Sixteen engine companies, five ladder companies, two aerial towers, and a heavy rescue company responded. The fire was contained by 4:30 p.m. Several crews, including Boston Fire Department Ladder 13 (my Dad's truck) and Engines 22 and 32, remained on the scene, performing cleanup. At 5:28 p.m., abruptly and without warning, all five floors of a section at the southeast corner of the building collapsed, burying 17 firefighters beneath a two-story pile of debris. Nine firefighters died: Thomas W. Beckwith, Joseph F. Boucher, Thomas J. Carroll, Charles E. Dolan, John E. Hanbury Jr., John E. Jameson, Richard B. Magee, Paul J. Murphy, and Joseph P. Saniuk. If my father had been scheduled to work that day, he probably would have died, too. He was lucky. Nine of his brother firefighters lay buried under the stone, glass, and twisted steel of the Vendome. My brothers and I were familiar with five of these men because they lived and worked as Dad in the same station house, Ladder 13 and Engine 22.

The Vendome tragedy was the worst firefighting disaster in Boston's history in terms of loss of life. My Dad's fire company, Ladder 13 and Engine 22, was among the first trucks to arrive at the fire. When Dad heard the news about the fire and building collapse, he ran from our house and directly to the scene to help with the recovery efforts. Afterward, he stayed at the firehouse, and we didn't see him for two days.

He dealt with the disaster the best he knew how: with whiskey. In those days, people often managed trauma by drinking and self-medicating to deal with their disappointments, hardships, and loss. That is exactly what Dad did in the firehouse and home that summer. These had been the men he shared the bunkhouse with, shared meals with, and talked about anything and everything, including life, love, their kids, the successes and failures of being the breadwinner, and the challenge of being a veteran adrift in a society that was increasingly hostile to veterans. Dad never talked about the Vendome, but occasionally, he would reminisce about one of the guys who died when the building collapsed. Maybe he had survivor guilt because I felt it was too much for him to discuss.

The year 1972 was probably the worst in my Dad's life, and it was far from over. In addition to trying to cope with the death of five of his closest friends, my Mom was rapidly losing her agonizing battle with cancer. She was the love of his life, and because alcohol had him by the throat, he continued to drink as he watched her slowly slip away. He was incapable of hiding his sorrow and sadness during these months. We all could see it—Big John's world was falling apart.

I located a visiting nursing service who would come to our home to administer daily morphine injections for my mother. The program, operated by the Daughters of Charity, offered home care assistance, including administering pain medication and the occasional sponge bath. But even with the Sisters' support, Mom's health steadily deteriorated. We could no longer care for her at home. From late August to December, Mom had no choice but to be in hospice in a state-run hospital.

Everyone in the family visited her frequently during these months. I tried to go there at least once daily, even for only a short visit. Sometimes, I borrowed Dad's car and drove my younger brothers to visit, but mostly I went alone. The visits were always sad, never knowing if it would be my last.

My father visited regularly and sat with her and talked. Sometimes, he was sober. Other times, he had been drinking. Mom never complained about his condition when he visited. She was grateful to see him. Openly talking about feelings and other emotions was not a regular practice in our family. Maybe their relationship transcended that, and they could communicate in their own way.

Toward the end of my mother's life, my father spent more time with her, as much as he could. One evening, when I visited her, I found my father there. Mom was heavily sedated and pretty much out of it. I noticed that Dad's hands were trembling, shaking from alcohol withdrawal. I had seen other men in my neighborhood who needed a drink to stop "the shakes," I could see he needed one. I asked him if he needed anything, but he replied no, thank you. It was around nine, and I knew the package stores would close soon, so I found a nearby store and bought a pint of whiskey. I returned to the hospital and handed him the bottle. I kissed my Mom goodnight as she lay unconscious and left her room, feeling ambivalent about what I had done. That was the only time I ever bought my father a drink in my entire life. My mother died four days later.

Mom was buried the day after Christmas. The wake was held on Christmas Eve and Christmas Day and was crowded with family, friends, and neighbors from the community. I didn't know what to do with myself, so I went to midnight Mass on Christmas Eve with friends. The local parish priest who was saying the Mass recognized me. At the end of the Mass, he nodded at me and called me over. I walked over, and he said, "How are you holding up, Burkie?"

I shook my head and said, "I don't know."

"Do you need anything? A few bucks, maybe?"

"No thanks," I said.

He replied, "If you need anything, come see me!"

I could tell he was sincere and meant what he said.

Christmas would never be the same again. After the holidays, we all tried our best to carry on with our lives—off to school for us kids and work for my older brothers and Dad. It was not an easy transition. I also regularly drank during this time and quickly developed a tolerance for more alcohol. I was smoking weed more frequently, too. People in our neighborhood were exceedingly kind and often offered to buy me a drink when I walked into the pub.

We were fortunate that our parents had made many friends. They all responded by helping us get on with our life without Mom. One neighbor, Mrs. Tobin, offered to mend our clothes when needed. She was a wonderful person. For many years after Mom passed, Mrs. Tobin told me how she looked forward to seeing Santa Clause in our window. We had an inexpensive plastic Santa that lit up at night. (I still have it.) I felt she wanted us to continue enjoying Christmas despite our sad feelings that time of year. When my brother asked why I was bothering to put up Christmas decorations, I told him it was for Mrs. Tobin. She looks forward to seeing that when she walks by, and I don't want to disappoint her. But it was really for me trying to hold on to some happy memories.

Another neighbor showed up with a laundry basket a few nights before school began. She let herself into the house and placed the basket in the corner of the living room, instructing us to put all the clothes that needed washing into the basket and that one of her daughters would come by to pick it up, returning everything cleaned and pressed. My brothers and I were sitting in the living room watching TV, and we told her, "That's okay, Mrs. Donlon. We're fine. We're all set."

"I'm not asking you. I'm telling you. Put the clothes in the basket!" she replied sternly, confidently. That was the camaraderie that existed in the housing project. We were incredibly grateful for everyone's kindness.

We all did the best we could under the circumstances. We pitched in to keep the house in order. I did most of the cooking and did my best to maintain the same weekly dinner schedule. But without our mother, we were lost souls. I regret that we never talked and processed Mom's death or how she lived her life. She was a beautiful and loving person who would give you her last dollar.

The Swim Meet

My final swim meet was in February of my senior year in high school, only two months after my Mom passed. We were having a solid season. My swimming had improved, and I was the co-captain of the team. Swimming was a great emotional relief, an escape from all the world's stress. I was in control of my environment and very comfortable when I swam. I was the only competitive swimmer in a house full of rabid hockey players.

"Don't you have a swim meet this week?" Dad asked me. "I overheard you tell your brother that you are competing."

"Yes, our final home meet is this Friday," I said, not providing details.

He said, "I'd love to come to see you swim. Where is it?"

"It's at the Southie Boys Club pool. But you don't have to go, and it's not a big deal." I purposely downplayed this event. In reality, it was an important swim meet, not only because it was my last competitive swim but also because it represented an opportunity for my school to improve in the city standings and might give me a chance to swim in college.

"I've never attended one of your swim meets, and I would really enjoy watching you."

A heck of a time to want to attend my swim meet, I thought. "No," I protested, "I don't want you there." I was getting nervous, and I sprinkled in some other flimsy excuses.

"Why not?" he asked.

"Because I don't want you showing up drunk." There. I said it.

"Don't be silly," he said. "I wouldn't do that. I want to watch."

"Listen to me," I shouted. "I do not want you there. If you show up, I'm walking out the door. You are not going to embarrass me in front of my friends." His response was a shocked look of disappointment and sadness. I stormed out of the house, ending the discussion.

I tried to focus on my swimming during the meet, but I was troubled, wondering whether he would come. I was so worried that he would show up, stumbling and drunk, that I had difficulty focusing on the competition. Fortunately, Dad did not make an appearance at the pool that day. I say, fortunately, but with a terrible ache and sadness in my heart. It would have meant the world to me to look up in the stands and see him there, cheering me on, clean and sober like a regular Dad, encouraging his son, sharing in my victory, and appreciating my hard work. Yet, more powerful, profound emotions, driven by fear and shame, denied us an opportunity to foster a healthy father-son relationship.

Years later, one of my younger brothers experienced the exact situation I had dreaded. Dad showed up at my brother's high school hockey practice intoxicated despite his promises not to. My brother was so upset at the sight of Dad, drunk in the stands, that he angrily slammed his hockey stick against the board and walked off, telling the coach he was done. The shame, embarrassment, and disappointment were too much for him to handle. My brother never played hockey again, abandoning an opportunity to play in college.

Seeing your dad drunk again and again and again is incomprehensibly devastating for a teenager. It is an ever-haunting nightmare to think that your father, the person you are supposed to look up to, is often a source of embarrassment—especially in the presence of your peers when teenage judgment is harsh. But what can be done to stop it? How can you deal with the shame and the hurt? What can you do when all you have seen at home is drinking?

Well, I decided you drink.

By the end of my senior year in high school, I drank excessively every weekend and on occasional weekdays. However, I believed I was controlling my alcohol consumption. In my mind, I was not about to become my father. *Never,* I told myself. It was a promise that I made many, many times. Unknowingly, the process of becoming an alcoholic was well underway. It already had a tight grip on me. All the unbearable memories and emotions disappeared when I drank. Foolishly, I drank more.

Working was a good distraction. It got me out of the house. Having a few dollars in my pocket gave me independence and security. It was a false sense of security because it never changed my situation at home. I also became the butt of my friends' ridicule as they accused me of being cheap and loving money. "Such a money-loving miser," my friends would tease me.

The truth was that money and the nice things it could buy didn't matter much. Neither did the satisfaction of a job well done. It was about stopping the pain and getting some control over my life. I did my best not to drown in this toxic environment. I concluded that life was cruel and that I could not rely on anyone, even the people I was supposed to love and who were supposed to love me. *I told myself not to trust anyone or show feelings if I wanted to succeed.* I had to work harder to escape the madness. I was determined to get on with my life and grow into adulthood.

I pledged that my life would be different. The best way to avoid emotional pain was to get an education, work hard, and never get married or have kids. At a time when most kids dream about what they want to be when they grow up, my goal was never to be an alcoholic! *The world is cruel, unfair, and painful. I'm going to be in control. I'm not going to contribute to this dysfunction. I will work harder and get as much education as possible. I will never bring a child into this world. And I will never be an alcoholic!* These are the things I repeatedly told myself as I justified my constant drinking.

One of the few things I did get right was that I recognized that I must have an education to escape the public housing project, acquire my own home, and prove I could succeed in life. This desire for an education motivated me to work harder. For some unknown reason, I believed obtaining a college degree was necessary to accomplish my goals. I may not have been an intellectually gifted student, but I knew I could work harder than most.

College and Night School

I graduated from high school that spring. Because some generous Boston public school teachers recommended me, I was awarded a full four-year scholarship to Boston University (BU). To be honest, academic expectations were low in my high school. When I landed at BU in September, I started to hang around local nightclubs in the area, continuing to drink regularly and smoke weed. As a result, my grades plummeted. I didn't believe that I had a problem with alcohol, but clearly, I did. Something was wrong with my academic abilities, but this was never addressed at home. My life experiences enabled me to overcome many hardships, but these skills did not transfer to what I needed to succeed in college. I didn't know how or who to ask for help. *Sink or swim* was my mantra.

I did not stop drinking because I did not believe it was a problem. I was having too much fun and was still young. Rather than study, I continued hanging with the guys on weekends. I did not make many friends at BU other than the few guys I drank with who hung out at the nearby nightclub. At the start of my sophomore year, I worked part-time at a nightclub near BU. This meant free drinks.

I decided to live on campus that semester, yearning for a change of scenery from living back in the neighborhood. I was on academic probation that semester and had to take some critical midterm exams. The evening before the exam, I drank alone in my room while other students crammed in the library. I had stolen a half-gallon of bourbon from another dorm room. The only thing that I had to mix it with was some root beer. I drank until I had a good buzz before passing out. The following day, I woke up with a vicious hangover and proceeded to walk to the building for the exam. Needless to say, I did poorly. Following the exam, I puked my guts out on Commonwealth Ave. The taste of root beer, bourbon, and whatever else was in my stomach permeated my nostrils. It was a horrible experience, and my idyllic college experience was quickly nearing its end.

By this time, my relationship with my father was practically nonexistent. I did not talk to him about college, failing grades, forfeiting my scholarship, or anything else. Our conversations were minimal and superficial, and I kept my distance. I could not stand being around him when he drank—and he drank every day. Because of my lack of funds, I had to live under the same roof, but we lived apart, and there was much stress.

I was told I had to withdraw from the full-time program early in my sophomore year. This meant losing my scholarship. I refused to take any responsibility for my behavior. I was angry at BU for rescinding my scholarship. The lifeline that would allow me a path to escape the housing project and live a comfortable life was gone.

Nevertheless, I was still determined to complete my college degree and investigated other possibilities. The dean's office informed me that I would be "allowed" to enroll in night school at Boston University at my own expense. I resolved that I would somehow take care of the cost of tuition myself. I did not want to ask my father for money. It may sound strange, but after so many heated shouting matches, I felt asking him for money would imply tacit approval of his behavior.

I worked full-time during the day and took evening classes. I decided to remain at BU because I did earn some academic credits and did not want to go through another application process. Living at home, with an active alcoholic, and working full-time while pursuing my college degree was extremely difficult, mainly because I was still drinking and partying. Sheer determination, huge resentment towards BU, and the fear of getting trapped in the project propelled me. I had one of those "I'll show them" attitudes, yet I was still miserable.

One evening, shortly after withdrawing from the daytime program at BU, I sat at the bar at one of my regular Southie hangouts. The bartender said, "I thought you were at BU. What are you doing here on a Tuesday night?"

Trying not to look ashamed and unable to be honest, my best response was, "I left BU. That place sucks."

He looked at me perplexed and said, "Hmmm." "I see," as he walked away. I could feel the judgment, but he decided to give me a pass and left my answer unchallenged, although his reaction stung!

The two years leading up to this were horrible. I lost my Mom to cancer and never had the opportunity to talk with anyone about her death or to process my emotions. I blew a full four-year scholarship to Boston University. I had no one to turn to and no clue how to understand what was happening inside me. I struggled to stay in the "here and now" or focus on the next task. I was lost without a compass and rapidly losing my sense of values. It's best not to talk about these things. There is too much shame. No one could ever truly understand.

I can only recall two occasions when anyone sincerely attempted to ask me what was happening in my life. The first was one evening when a verbal blowout between my parents emotionally shook me. When I went to hang out with my friends, one pal could see the anger, pain, and sadness on my face. He came closer, looked into my eyes, and anxiously asked, "Tim, what happened to you?" I shook my head as he asked again, "What's wrong, man? What happened?"

I desperately wanted to tell him what had happened. But fear, humiliation, and shame prevented me from reaching for a lifeline.

"Nothing," I said. If things looked terrible on the outside, it was much worse on the inside. My emotions were in an internal toxic brew. All I wanted to do was to die and for all this to end. *Please, God, make it stop.* Nothing more was said as the other guys appeared, one by one, as we talked, laughed, smoked cigarettes, and enjoyed a joint or two. I pretended that things were fine and had some beers. And that was it, as though nothing happened at home that day.

The second time was when an academic counselor at BU asked to speak to me about my failing grades. He was a psychologist and wanted to explore possible reasons for my poor performance. During our brief conversation, he asked about things at home. "What is your living situation? Are things okay?"

I briefly told him about my Mom passing away and how much I missed her. "I'm fine," I said. I ignored any questions about my Dad other than to say, "he likes his tea"—an old Irish saying I used to describe someone who drinks too much.

"Is it a particular brand of tea?"

"Yes, it's whiskey," I said with a smile. I probably came off as a wise-ass punk. In reality, I was burdened with interior shame and fear and incapable of accepting help even though I needed it badly.

"Oh, I see," he said. He changed the subject and went on to ask about my college experience. I told him that I felt my family and community life was being taken away from me and replaced with something else. My views broadened as I was exposed to other possibilities and ways to experience the world. Looking back, I understand that it was impossible for me to talk about something so painful and to try to describe or even explain it to another person. But that was the only time I remember coming close to talking to anyone about my situation at home. I could not persuade BU to let me stay in school full-time or allow me to use my scholarship toward the evening program at BU. I received a direct firm "No" without an opportunity to appeal. I was on my own if I wanted to attend college. I knew that I must obtain an education to get ahead in life. *Fuck them. I'll show them,* I thought.

Regardless, I continued taking classes while making time to work and party. I had to work to pay for my tuition. My friends and I spent summer weekends on Cape Cod, which was always a summer-long binge-drinking party. I was an active and willing participant. Certainly, nobody was holding me down and forcing alcohol down my throat. I was in the midst of a series of poor decisions and becoming the alcoholic, I said I would never become.

Fortunately, I was hired as a transitional aide at South Boston High School, where I had graduated two years earlier. This was during the turbulent period of federal-mandated forced busing in Boston. Busing created fear and anger by radically changing the status quo. What was covert racism now became overt hatred, accelerating deeply rooted animosity across the city. I walked the school's halls to maintain the peace between local kids and bused-in kids from Roxbury. The social experiment of pitting poor Black and poor White kids against each other was depressing and disappointing to witness, and I had a front-row seat.

The Boston University professors and predominantly suburban BU students followed the news coverage of this social experiment. My professors were staunch, vocal proponents of forced busing—for other children—while their children attended elite private schools. My knowledge from working as a transitional aide provided me with plenty of exciting experiences to discuss in class. Most of my professors and fellow students acquired their information on the evening news. At the same time, I received mine from direct sources.

In the high school where I worked, I made friends with Black and White students and staff and earned a solid reputation for being fair and helpful to all. But back at BU, I was perceived as a bigot simply because of where I lived. In fact, it felt like they were convinced I was incapable of not being a racist because of where I came from. That kind of narrow-mindedness infuriated me. Often, I felt as though my opinions were neither noteworthy nor wanted. To many of my professors and peers at BU, I was nothing but a white Irish bigot from South Boston. It did not matter how respectfully I treated both Black and White students at work. Being from South Boston was a sign to many that I must be an uneducated, ignorant racist. I labored on, determined to get my college degree despite the unfriendly environment I found myself in.

Prejudice was not limited to poverty and race. Some of the professors I had at BU were openly anti-Catholic. I recall sitting in a large auditorium with students before Christmas when one of the professors on the stage remarked, "Christmas is arriving soon. As you know, it was a Virgin birth." He rolled his eyes and smirked, saying, "Can you imagine a Virgin birth." Laughing with another professor in front of the assembly, he said, "Now that's something, wouldn't you say?" None of the other adults in the room challenged him. After that display, I lost respect for most BU professors for openly mocking my religious beliefs. I might be personally angry with God, but laughing at another person's religious beliefs seemed inexcusable, in my opinion. I walked away on that day, deciding that my degree was nothing more than a business transaction. I did not care for these people; they certainly didn't care about me. *I will earn my degree and move on.*

Although I desperately wanted to be part of college life at BU, I did not feel any connection to the university or other students. My delayed emotional development and lack of preparation were evident to me and others. I also had a noticeable vocabulary gap, which hindered my ability to fit in at BU. Even my Boston accent, often mocked, was a constant reminder of my upbringing and shortcomings. I later discovered that this is a familiar feeling for many inner-city kids who attend greater Boston colleges.

I have to give myself credit for keeping an open mind, which broadened my views and opened up the world of possibilities, even though it was very challenging at times. I did feel like I was losing a sense of who I was by attending college. Still, I was changing my views and gaining insight into other possibilities and opportunities. This also made me feel superior to those condescending elitist haters who dismissed me because of who I was and where I was from, making the value of my education so much more important.

Summer Cop

When I was twenty years old, I noticed "summer cops" working for the various towns on Cape Cod. These were seasonal positions, typically filled by college guys who wanted a future career in law enforcement. I thought that was cool and planned to apply for the job the following summer. As it happened, because of some political connections, I did indeed get the job as a summer cop on Cape Cod that next year. Some guys who drank in the same bar that I did knew a guy who knew a guy…that's how these things sometimes work.

So, I was twenty-one years old, drinking heavily, using weed, walking Main Street Hyannis at night in a police officer's uniform, and packing a .38 revolver. It does not get any better than that! Friends asked me if I was frightened of being a cop on Cape Cod. I would say, "No, because I'm armed and dangerous. I'm not the one that should be afraid." That was true! Partying on the Cape during the summer with a badge and a gun made me armed and dangerous. I carried my police department badge with me whenever I was out drinking. Flashing the badge allowed my friends and me to cut the line and avoid the cover charge at many nightclubs on the Cape. Best of all, the "shield" was a sure way to avoid getting arrested if I was driving under the influence of alcohol. I was frequently driving while drinking, just like my Dad often did, but I did not take notice of it at that time.

I had a solid reputation as a good worker in the department, but I was also known as a big party guy. I kept a cooler full of ice-cold beer and a couple of joints in my car. I could not wait to get off work after my weekend shift to run back and join the party. If the cops came, which they occasionally did, I told them I lived there and that my friends would keep the noise down.

Late one evening, after returning from work, a few of my friends sat at the kitchen table in our cottage, drinking and smoking weed with new friends they had met at a club in town. Wearing my uniform, I walked in and yelled, "Don't anybody move!"

One of my friends stood up. I pushed him against the wall, saying I'd break his head open if he moved. I shouted, "Where's the fucking weed?"

The guys who did not know me sat in shock as I instructed all my buddies, now in on the prank, to get up against the wall.

"Who has the weed?" I shouted. One of my friends pointed to one of the guys they had just met.

I shouted, "Give me that weed, or you're going to jail!" He handed me the weed, and I said, "Where are the rolling papers?"

He almost cried and said, "I only got a pipe."

I took the pipe from him, filled it with weed, and started to smoke. I told this guy the stuff tasted like ragweed, passed his pipe to one of my buddies, and asked him what he thought.

We all started laughing at these guys, and I retreated to my bedroom to get out of my uniform. Every night was one big party, and I loved it.

I almost gave myself up when two summer cops brought a young guy into the station at the end of one of my shifts. I asked what he did. One of the cops held up a bag of weed and said they had found this on him and had placed him under arrest. I said, "Wow, you're kidding me, right? That's nothing. Let him go. He's just a kid."

While they were booking him, I decided to intervene. I walked into the sergeant's office to speak up for this young man. The sergeant was a streetwise cop who spent his leisure time in a motorcycle club on Cape Cod. He had seen me in action, partying on the Cape, keeping up with his biker buddies, doing shots, and shooting beers. There were some bad dudes at these biker parties, and I was sure lots of marijuana was available. I pleaded with the sergeant to let the kid go, "You know that kid out there will get screwed. Sarge, for Christ's sake, I got that much weed in my ashtray." *Oops.*

He shook his head and said, "Yeah, but he got caught, and you didn't. Now get the fuck out of my office."

The thought of getting arrested passed through my mind, and for some reason, I realized how serious this was. I stopped smoking weed and never smoked it again. I was twenty-two years old and had enjoyed a wonderful seven-year run.

After being a summer cop on the Cape for two seasons, I was offered a full-time job as a patrolman. When I told the lieutenant I was declining because I wanted to return to college to finish, he was surprised that I did not already have a degree. I did not take the time to explain why I did not have my degree. Besides, who wants to live on the Cape during the winter when the place is dead? I wanted to be back home, partying with my friends, and continue taking night classes.

College and beyond

I continued to work and attend school at night. I had various full and part-time jobs, including lifeguard, skate guard, teacher's aide, bartender, and bouncer. During football season, I was a photographer for a local film lab. I filmed local high school football games on Saturdays. After the games, I helped process the films and readied them for distribution the next day. It was good money for watching a football game.

I could finally move out of my father's house and rent an apartment with a friend's brother. I took another step, determined to make it on my own. The apartment was a simple, sparsely furnished two-bedroom in a twelve-unit building in Quincy. A twenty-minute ride from South Boston, I drove four or five times a week to hang out back home with my friends. I did not know any neighbors in the building or the neighborhood. For the first time in my life, I was locking my front door. We never locked our doors in the project—there was never any need to. I didn't even have a key. It sounds strange because of all the insanity that existed, but the project had a certain sense of security. I knew all the players, and if anything happened, they would protect me.

During this time, I was going it alone. After work, I would stop in the bar to see the guys, then head home to an empty apartment. I rarely saw my roommate, who also worked full-time. There was no need to socialize with each other. He did not drink much, which I thought was strange, and we did not have much in common. He grew up in the suburbs, and I was a city kid.

Working and studying gave me a sense of purpose and control. However, I wasn't enjoying life or deeply interested in college. I was going through the motions, accomplishing a task I was driven to complete. It was an unpleasant daily routine. Work, study, drink. Work, study, drink.

After four years of night school and summer semesters, I earned a degree in business administration from Boston University. I had paid for my education and supported myself. I was not going to owe anyone. I was not going to put myself in the position of having my father ever be able to say that he had helped me get my degree.

My father attended my graduation ceremony, and we went out for dinner with a couple of my brothers. Another BU student who graduated received a beautiful sports car as a gift from his parents, a gleaming silver Bricklin with gullwing doors, parked on Commonwealth Avenue for all to see. Just as Dad, my brothers, and I walked by, the graduate's mother handed him the keys as she shouted how proud she was of her baby. Dinner at an average restaurant and a firm handshake was my graduation gift.

I decided to throw my own graduation party at a disco nightclub where I worked as a bartender. I rented the place and had an open bar for all my friends and anyone who wanted to join in. We partied all night, and it was a blast! This was a great graduation party! My friends gave me graduation gifts of cash, which I used to pay off the bar bill. I think I broke even and viewed my graduation party as another example of my independence.

Despite all I had accomplished and the obstacles I had overcome, my graduation from college felt hollow. I was constantly struggling and racing to prove something throughout my college years. I'm unsure what I was searching for or what I thought I was missing in my life. I knew I had propelled myself across the finish line based solely on determination, drive, and a huge resentment.

Eventually, I saved enough money to buy a small two-family house. It needed a lot of work, but I was born and raised in public housing, so I was proud of this accomplishment. I had achieved two of my goals: obtaining a college degree and owning a home.

I have now turned my attention to improving my job situation. I was employed as an auditor for Massport, the state authority operating the Port of Boston and Logan Airport. My job was to check the number of flights and types of aircraft that landed and took off. The street where I grew up, Logan Way, was named for the same US General for whom the airport is named.

I went to see my state senator, William Bulger, brother of the infamous Whitey. Because his family had lived near us in the project, they remained family friends. My parents and other families in the project were involved in the Bulger campaign when William first ran for office as a state representative. Many organizational parties were held at our house, which was always filled with political signs, bumper stickers, flyers, and envelopes for literature mailings in an election year. Many women from the project sat at our kitchen table and hand-addressed envelopes for mailing to the voters in the district.

William Bulger never forgot where he came from or the people who helped him get elected. When I told him I was unhappy at Massport, he offered me a job with the Post Audit and Oversight Committee in the State House—that day! He was the Senate President at the time. Because I had been working as an auditor, it seemed like a natural fit, but I doubt I would have been hired had it not been for those political connections. One more example of one project guy helping another.

On the first day of work in the State House, I was told by the chief of staff that it would "behoove" me to use the opportunity to get an advanced degree, such as in Law or maybe an MBA. I decided to return to Boston University and work on a master's degree in urban affairs. It was explained that I should acquire an advanced degree if I ever wanted to distinguish myself, have more responsibility, and make more money. One more thing he said, "Start looking for a real job. This position in the state house will not last forever!" This was good advice because I observed that once your sponsor was out, so were you! I witnessed a person's desk be moved out of their office into a smaller office the day after his sponsor lost his re-election bid in a primary election. This seemed heartless to me because three months were remaining in the term. When I asked why they were doing that? He said, "One day, you're a peacock, and the next day you're a feather duster." Another one of life's lessons.

Working in the city with people with similar backgrounds was a strong pull for me, so urban planning sounded like a great option. BU offered this as a master's degree program, and I knew I could handle attending evening classes. I still harbored resentment toward BU and thought of this as just another business transaction.

I began to attend graduate school at night. As I had done before, I took evening classes while working full-time during the day. Occasionally, I picked up a few hours of bartending or other part-time jobs. Of course, I also made time to party with my buddies. Once again, work, study, and drink. I was in a vicious cycle because the social aspect of my life was vital to me. My friends were what kept me going. I had so much fun and felt comfortable and accepted in the group. I was at ease with the guys—something I rarely felt or experienced at home.

On paper, everything seemed picture-perfect. I had a full-time government job and owned my own house. I worked toward a master's degree, engaged in sports and recreation, and attended various social events. I was active in local politics, a member of the Democratic ward committee, and a member of the Knights of Columbus.

As I was doing it all, I continued to drink regularly. I am sure I would have done much better in school had I consumed less alcohol and studied more. Although I had a good-paying job with responsibility and was sure I was competent at my job, I probably was not a good employee. How productive can you be when you show up for work hungover from the night before? When I was drinking, studying seemed less important, as did networking, relationships, and a career. I pushed those things aside during both undergraduate and graduate school. Who has time to socialize and network when there is work and drinking to do? I thought all the socializing and networking I needed could be found at the bar. Occasionally, I would meet with a fellow student after class for a drink.

If you drank as I did, chances are that we grew up in a similar neighborhood and had a lot in common. I was jealous of my brothers, who developed a vast network of close friendships during their college years that remain connected with them today. I began to understand that putting work and drinking first came at a tremendous personal cost.

Most nights, class ended at nine sharp, and afterward, I often headed to the bar to watch a hockey or football game with my buddies from the projects. One evening, my professor ran a little over wrapping up his lecture. I suddenly closed my book, stood up, and announced, "It's 9 p.m. Class is over. Good night." The entire class was in shock as I walked out the door. In my mind, I thought I was right and the only one with enough guts to say so. I pictured all the other students looking at me as I walked into the bar. What I did not realize then was that, once again, my actions were motivated by an obsession to drink. When I wasn't drinking, I was thinking about it. I needed to get to that bar and have a beer! The following week, two of my fellow students commented that I had a lot of balls to get up and leave like that. "It must have been important," one of them said.

"Yes, it was very important," I replied.

After two years of night and summer classes, I earned my Master of Urban Affairs from Boston University. Again, determination and drive enabled me to obtain the degree. There was no celebration or party, only a handshake and congratulations. I had paid for my education myself by working hard and drinking hard. It wasn't easy, but willpower, self-reliance, and resiliency saw me through. Not bad for a kid who had been held back in the second and fifth grades and transferred in the ninth grade because of poor academics. On the outside, I was beaming with pride, but yet again, the accomplishment felt like a hollow victory.

The degree did anchor me, giving me the confidence to take risks and apply for positions with more responsibility and compensation. I had been told that having an advanced degree would open more doors for me, which it did. I landed a Planning and Development job working for the same agency that owned and operated the public housing I once lived in. I was excited to have the opportunity to help people like myself have a safe and secure place to live.

I did not have a life plan, and I certainly did not have a role model. My pursuit of education was a way out of the project. Certain questions gnawed at my insides: *Had I chased this degree to make up for something that happened in my past? Was I only operating out of fear and loss? Did I need some sense of control in my life?* It felt less like an accomplishment and more like a burden to conquer. I had been working and drinking so much that I did not have time to enjoy what I was learning or get to know my classmates. I was moving fast but going nowhere. Life was rushing by, and I felt like I was skimming across the surface of my life. Indeed, I was not an active participant in it.

Working as a way to cope and control.

A happy life consists not in the absence of hardships, but in the mastery of hardships.
-Helen Keller

Neighbors and friends were so kind to my family and me when my mother passed away. I could have taken advantage of this kindness by parlaying self-pity to get an easy ride. Instead, I found relief in work because work allowed me to feel valued and have a sense of purpose and control. In every job that I had, a supervisor or co-worker would say. "Great job, Tim!" It was not always that way, and I certainly was not always a stellar employee, but it felt great when it happened, and I could hold my head high. A paycheck or a large tip when bartending meant more than the money. But it was not about the extra cash. Compliments and accolades were a measurement of how I was as a person. How I felt about myself was based on what others thought about me. Looking back at the futility of this habit of working, I missed out on so much in life.

I recently looked at my Social Security statement and noticed that I started paying into Social Security when I was fourteen. I had several jobs in my early teens. Most of these jobs were for cash, "under the table." Others were not. I delivered papers, shoveled snow, and helped at the machine shop across the street from my house. At sixteen, I was a busboy in an officer's club at a local navy base. It was here that I started to steal drinks and bottles of wine with other guys from South Boston.

Working was a much-needed distraction and got me out of the house and away from the madness. It was a diversion from the anxiety I experienced as a kid. I helped out in the small machine shop on our street for hours to avoid going home, but I didn't know how to explain the meaning of this at the time. However, because the situation at home never changed, it was a false sense of security. Looking back, I think I missed many opportunities to be a kid. I never sat back to see the beauty in things around me or enjoy simple things in life.

Many years later, I met a man from Boston while on vacation in Florida. He said that he was a retired Boston Firefighter. I told him my Dad also was a Boston Firefighter. "What's your name, and where are you from," he asked. I told him Burke from South Boston. " Big John Burke Ladder 13," he asked. We discovered he had known my father as they were firefighters on Ladder 13. He then said the same thing that everyone says. "What a great guy your dad was!" He asked, "Which one are you?" I told him my name, and he recalled talking with my father about my desire to work. "Geez, he's a young kid. Why doesn't he want to play like the other kids in the summertime? Why does he want to work?" The guy said they sat around drinking coffee for hours but could never figure it out. I had mixed emotions when he told me this. I never imagined I would be the topic of conversation at the firehouse. I wished I had had that conversation with my Dad as a kid.

Working served two purposes for me. It gave me some control and allowed me not to ask my father for money. I did not want to be indebted to him for anything, fearing that he would throw it in my face. I also had to consider that someday he would like something in return. This is another example of my "all or nothing" thinking, a pattern I developed as a result of growing up in a dysfunctional home.

My work and all my jobs were about control and independence. It was never about the money. Work provided consistency, a purpose, a routine, stability, and a reward at the end of the week. I can see why and how work provided a better way of living. Was this the correct way to live my life? I don't know.

But just like alcohol, feeling appreciated on the job worked until it did not.

I talked with a former neighbor a few years ago and informed him I had retired from my full-time job. He looked at me and said, "Yeah, sure. How many jobs do you have left?"

"Two," I answered, "but they're both part-time jobs." This was true. I was appointed to a Planning Board for the City and worked a few hours each week as a therapist.

He laughed as he walked away and said, "You're never going to retire. It's not in you."

His comment made me uncomfortable and caused me to take an honest look at myself. That guy was right. I have worked way too much! Even now, work helps me feel safe and independent. But from what? Life is not about work, and I need to change. I am a recovering workaholic and alcoholic, trying to keep the peace and live spiritually. I need to learn to let go and enjoy life. Most of my free time is devoted to travel and recreation, swimming, sailing, and pickleball, and I love it! Soon, I will be fully retired...maybe!

Intro to a Family Support Group

My Dad's drinking never stopped or even slowed down. Each day began with the hope that things would change, but it was always more of the same. My Mom was not there to be his support and hold him even somewhat accountable. He was a lonely, sad man in the grip of alcoholism. My brothers and I tried to get him to stop drinking without success. My brothers attempted to use love and compassion to get him to change; regrettably, I occasionally used threats and shame. Our efforts were to no avail. Nothing we did or none of his painful experiences had any effect on motivating him to seek help.

A former neighbor and friend of my parents, Mary, who was aware of my Dad's struggle with alcohol, invited me to attend a family support meeting. I decided to accept her offer and attend a Friday night meeting. I was afraid I might be asked to speak, so I sat in the back of the room, keeping my guard up and avoiding eye contact. But I listened carefully. I immediately identified with the speakers. These people had the same experiences my family had and spoke honestly about the details. What I considered shameful topics, which I kept buried inside myself and ate away at me, were being discussed in the open. It was an eye-opening experience! Mary's presence provided a sense of safety as she sat near me silently, offering support.

Because these people had lived through what I had, they understood my reluctance. They knew how to invite me into the group without making me feel panicky or running for the door. They knew what a dysfunctional home was like because they had lived through it. They survived and came out the other side, finding peace and contentment.

People were kind. A simple "Hello Tim, it's good to see you" always felt good. "I hope to see you next week," one woman said. "Keep coming; we need you." I wanted to cry when I heard that.

I became remarkably comfortable at the family meetings, learning about hope and taking new risks of letting someone inside my head and sharing the shameful secrets I'd been concealing for so long. I was not alone, and these strangers, who understood my secrets, were willing to help me. They wanted nothing in return but for me to find peace and acceptance. I went for two years, and I learned a lot. I realized that I could do things to take care of myself and, more importantly, let go of things I could not control. I learned that the only thing I could change and was responsible for was myself and my reactions to my father's alcoholism. I knew that children who experience traumatic incidents at the hands of an active alcoholic frequently have distressing flashbacks of the psychological and physical abuse perpetrated against them. Research shows that these experiences lead to numerous chronic emotional problems such as depression, alcohol abuse, obsessive-compulsive disorder, anxiety, an altered sense of self, and difficulties forming healthy relationships.

I would later learn that repeated exposure to early trauma can leave lasting marks on a child's brain. These are critical times in childhood development. Children only have one opportunity to develop into healthy adults. When it goes wrong, as it did in my childhood home, the results may be long-lasting and directly related to the trajectory an individual's life will take. These changes to the developing brain impact memory skills, learning and retention, and emotional regulation.

Parents who drink excessively often minimize the impact and deny the effect that their alcoholism has on their kids. They would rather defend their right to drink at any cost. Alcoholics harm their family members more than anyone else. However, an active alcoholic would never see or admit that they have caused significant damage to the people they should love the most. The saddest part of all of this is that it is all preventable!

When I attended the family support group, I was focused on my Dad's drinking problem, not my own. I told myself I did not have a problem. Ironically, following the meetings, I typically went to the bar to hang out with my friends, totally oblivious to my drinking patterns. *I don't have a problem. My Dad does. He needs to change, not me!*

Dad's Demise

Twelve years had passed since my Mom died and the Vendome Hotel catastrophe. Dad was fortunate not to be on duty that day, but in many ways, he also lost his life that day. I can only imagine my father's thoughts about the Vendome Hotel tragedy. It overshadowed his happy memories of his wedding reception in the same ballroom where nine of his brother firefighters lost their lives. How cruel that the place of my parents' hopeful happiness became the site of unspeakable heartbreak and horror.

Dad never recovered from these losses. He was gripped by alcoholism, stuck in a daily rut of drinking at home or the nearby VFW post. Love and happy memories could not conquer this firefighter's emotional pain. Was the pain too severe, too intense for him to overcome? Alcohol must have provided the only, albeit temporary, relief. Getting through each day must have been a struggle for Big John.

Gazing into his eyes, I could see he was a broken man. His dreams of spending his golden years with the love of his life and watching his six boys grow up and have their own families vanished. Friends would ask, "How's your dad doing?" This was always followed by, "He's a great guy." People knew he had had some difficult years, and I am sure some had an inkling of the depth of his struggles. Although they knew he had a drinking problem, it was never acknowledged or discussed.

After my Mom passed, my brothers and I were melancholy and at a loss for options as we watched our Dad slowly drink himself to death. We tried many times to get him help, but he was not capable of receiving it. We felt terrible sadness for him and never mistreated or disrespected him. Even so, I could never forgive or accept his alcoholism either. I could not forgive him because I did not know how or where to start. What good would it do? *We cannot undo the past,* I thought. *It is what it is.*

A healthy father-son relationship was only a dream. I would have given anything to be able to go to my Dad with a problem, have a thoughtful discussion, and together come up with a solution. It was not to be. I no longer wanted to hurt my Dad like I had when I was younger. I pitied his painfully lonely existence. Because it was impossible to get past the trauma of the past or the continued drinking, I vacillated between "it's his decision to drink, and that's what happens" and "I wish the poor guy would get some help and enjoy his remaining years." During the years after Mom's passing, he often sat alone in the dark in his bedroom, drinking whiskey while listening to an inexpensive portable AM radio and smoking cigarettes. Witnessing his painful downfall was difficult for everyone who cared about him.

Today, I understand that the disease of alcoholism destroyed my Dad's ability to control his drinking. Alcoholism wanted him to be intoxicated and isolated, and it succeeded. When I visited, I kept my conversations to a minimum, maintaining a relationship with him only more out of loyalty to my Mom than hoping to enjoy some father-and-son relationship. This entire drawn-out situation was difficult for my brothers as well. I could see that Dad wanted to talk about my life, career, friends, and challenges—all things a proud father wants to discuss with his children. But I could not speak with him when he was intoxicated. It brought up too many painful memories. One-word sentences were my replies to his questions. I was being polite and going through the motions while staying on guard. I had a legitimate fear that our discussions would result in a hurtful argument.

Sometimes, I could see that he desperately wanted to experience the joy and pride of my success, but I couldn't handle it. In many ways, we were both broken by the disease of alcoholism. How much I wanted to tell him my stories, how much I had accomplished, and what brought me happiness. But I did not know how to talk with him. It was like when I was a kid and wanted to tell him how my swimming was going and how I had won a couple of races. But I was never comfortable enough to do so. I could not sit with my abuser for a conversation without emotionally re-experiencing past events.

I genuinely wanted his wisdom and guidance for life's challenges. But I could not get past his drinking. I ignored my excessive drinking. *I have my drinking under control. Also, I don't have a wife and kids, so I'm not hurting anyone as he did.*

Some part of me knew that a relationship was there for him and me, yet I did not know how to find it. It was just not within my reach. My last conversation with my Dad was after my youngest brother Brian asked me to check in on him. Brian was the last one living in the house with Dad. He was concerned that Dad did not look well and needed medical attention. I called Dad that afternoon. He sounded as though he had been drinking. I urged him to see his doctor. "Brian's worried about you," I said. "We all are. How about going to the doctor for Brian? Would you do that?"

He said he was fine and just needed to take a nap.

Then, for some unknown reason, I said something I had not told him in many years. I surprised myself when I said, "Dad, we may not say it or show it enough, but we all love you and do not want to see anything happen to you. So please go to the doctor."

There was a long silence. A hopeless, desolate silence. Neither of us was equipped to say anything more, but I believe I touched him in a good way.

"Thank you, Tim," he said. "I'll talk to Brian when he gets home and make the appointment."

"Okay," I said. "Call me if you need anything. Any one of us will drive you to the doctor's office."

The following day, on August 9, 1984, he was dead. Big John died alone in his bedroom in that project apartment that had started with so much hope and promise. The same project apartment where he raised six boys and lived with the woman he loved. He died not just from a massive heart attack but also from a broken heart. He died alone, without anyone holding his hand as he passed, desperately alone while under the spell and control of alcoholism. Booze took him as it took his values, hopes, dreams, and loved ones. Everything he had cherished was gone, and he died alone.

A few days later, it seemed the entire community turned out at his funeral. The church was overflowing, with many people standing outside. Members of the fire department and many elected officials, including the mayor, our local congressman, and the president of the Massachusetts State Senate, attended the funeral. Officers from the police department, people from the youth hockey league, and several of my teachers from my high school attended the service. Everyone came to pay their respects to Big John. Several older Black women from the South End of Boston who lived near the firehouse also came to pay their respects. Mind you, this was not a good time to show your face in segregated South Boston if you were Black because of the violence over the busing situation. They did, and my brothers and I were incredibly grateful for their gracious gesture. We each made it a point to shake the hands of these women and thanked them for the respect they showed our Dad. The size of the crowd was a testament to how well-liked my Dad was in the community and how much he was respected. I believe this big send-off was a tribute to the elusive good guy, which was the most significant part of who my Dad was.

I knew this day would come and thought I was prepared. But I was not. I cried inconsolably for three days during the wake and funeral. At the time, I thought it was strange that his death affected me so profoundly. I believed that I was hardened by my childhood experiences and emotionally detached from him. From a young age, I had always been confident that all my problems would be over once he was gone, and I would get on with my life. Problem solved by Mother Nature. The trail of devastation will come to an end. Was I ever wrong. My troubles, my nightmare, had only begun on the day he died.

The Tragic Reality of Firefighters and First Responders

What a heartbreaking and inglorious way for a hero to die. I continue to admire firefighters as heroes who place their lives at risk each day with courage and honor. I am confident that none of my dad's peers, friends, or family wanted his life to end this way. I believe enabling his alcoholism played a crucial role in his tragic, unfortunate demise. I cannot help but think of what might have happened if someone or something had interrupted my dad's drinking early in his life. It is possible that some type of pause would have resulted in a moment of clarity for him. What if my Mom did go to the fire commissioner to report his drinking while on duty? Would he have stopped the on-the-job drinking prevalent in those days? Would a warning, with consequences, from someone with authority have put the brakes on the attitude of entitlement many held toward alcohol use and abuse? What if his supervisors did their job better? I was not the only one to see this drastic personality change when he drank alcohol. I say this because active alcoholism and drug abuse are more rampant now than ever in our society. According to several reliable sources who work in the treatment field, substance abuse on the job continues today, just not as overtly. We will never know just how many families are living in fear of an active substance abuser. I wished someone from the firehouse had asked me what I thought about Dad's drinking while on the job and what actions should have been taken.

The people with authority who allowed him to drink with impunity and looked the other way did not help him. They abandoned him. His drinking buddies did not help him in his time of need. They were not true friends. They were a force that usurped his moral compass when he desperately needed a correction toward the truth. Dad needed and rightfully deserved a sober friend to help him; all he ended up with was booze. Booze was his companion when he died. The day after he passed, I went into his bedroom and found a half pint of whiskey in its usual hiding spot in the dresser, under his boxer shorts.

I also had my drinking buddies I drank with. I had a strong attachment to these friends and would kill for them if it ever came to that. They were guys I looked to for companionship and support or when I needed an excuse to drink. My friends told me when I was depressed, "Have a drink—you'll feel better." They never questioned my motivations when I was falling down drunk. They would do "shots" with me and get hammered for the sake of getting hammered.

I lost count of how many times someone had walked up to me and asked about my father, often saying what a good man he was. I always questioned how we could be talking about the same person. Many times, I wanted to scream the truth that my father was a violent drunk who tormented us and made our lives utterly miserable. People know little about what occurs in someone else's home or inside another person's mind. They have no idea of the pain, stress, and anxiety someone may be causing or experiencing. Paradoxically, they often hold that person in high regard and even express admiration. This was the case with those who knew my father, making these encounters awkward and uncomfortable.

Even James "Whitey" Bulger admired and respected my Dad. He would often inquire, "How's your Dad? He's one of the good guys. Always a gentleman! Every time I see him walking home from work, I think, what a great guy!" Like everyone else, Jimmy witnessed what was on the outside—a hard-working blue-collar guy with two jobs, a firefighter and a truck driver, who returned home after a long, hard day of work. What's not to respect? I cite this example because it's from a notorious alleged sociopath who could see the humanity in a man that I could not. I often wondered: *Am I that broken?*

After many years as a clinical social worker and therapist, I now understand what firefighters and other first responders must handle professionally. Their jobs are complicated and demanding, often involving rapid life-and-death decisions. In those days, as I've said, they didn't have proper protective equipment, and building fire codes didn't provide safe structures as they do today.

Firefighters also witness traumatic events with great regularity. They often have to remove the bodies of adults and children burned to death. They bear the self-doubt that they could have saved a life—if only! Undoubtedly, my Dad had undiagnosed and untreated trauma. Back then, no support systems were in place, such as employee assistance programs or critical incident debriefings. PTSD was not even a diagnosis. The only "solution" for many was alcohol, which the supervisors tolerated and sometimes tacitly encouraged. Like most alcoholics, he needed help, not accolades.

When my Dad was at home and a neighbor needed emergency help, he was the one who responded. On at least three occasions, neighbors ran to our house because someone had a heart attack. On one occasion, a woman who lived in the building across from us fell out of a second-floor window and came crashing down on the asphalt. My Dad rushed to help her until the police arrived with a "Paddy Wagon" to transport her to the hospital. In those days, they did not have ambulances with EMTs as we do today to respond to medical emergencies. The quickest way to get to the hospital was on a stretcher in the back of the wagon.

I was oblivious to the trauma my father experienced because of these incidents. Today, we know those first responders pay a massive price with their emotional and physical health, resulting in a closed culture in which brother firefighters can trust only each other for support. Unfortunately, alcohol abuse plays an enormous role in self-medication to cope with the emotional struggles of this type of job. First responders must deal with fear, self-doubt, helplessness, disappointments, poor self-care, untreated trauma, and shame, to name a few significant emotional issues.

But, as we know, the first responder's job often changes them; sadly, they don't see it. If they do, they do not have a solution. Repeated exposure to critical incidents will affect the first responders' personalities—and not in a positive way. We also know that these incidents result in a much higher rate of suicide for first responders. Men and women caught up in this cycle often have poor relationships with their families and appear angry and distant. The result? More self-medication and alcohol dependency.

My Dad was a proud professional firefighter who returned from World War II military service. This "greatest generation" was always humble about their heroic efforts, whether in the war or rescuing someone from a burning building and saving lives. That humility is one of the things I respect and miss from the older generations. I rarely see that humility today.

Unfortunately, the skills that made them good at their jobs did not transfer to their personal lives. In a battle to survive, alcohol might seem like a solution—until it is not. Trauma exposure often leads to stress, anxiety, depression, and more alcohol, exacerbating existing emotional damage. I can see that my Dad had alcohol dependency and untreated depression. He also had permission to drink while on duty without consequences, which did not help his mental health. When you don't step in and stop the behavior, you become part of the problem.

In 1972, after losing nine brother firefighters, and his wife, he sank into a much deeper depression. Alcohol was his only option, a necessity for him to cope. The disease of alcoholism had him by the throat and never let go until the day he died, a painfully lonely death. He was never free from the heavy chains of alcoholism.

My Drinking Life

I was thirty years old when my Dad passed away. I was at that time what I would describe as a "functioning chronic drinker." For the next six years, my alcohol use continued to increase, progressing rapidly to the point that it could be described "as out of control."

I started abusing alcohol and smoking weed when I was fifteen. Drinking was a normal part of growing up in Southie, and as a community, we normalized alcohol use and abuse; seemingly, everyone abused alcohol. Or so we thought. It was present at every social get-together—christenings, birthday parties, weddings, funerals, and always when someone joined or returned from the military. I honestly felt awkward if I didn't have a drink in my hand when I was with friends. On more than one occasion, when I declined a beer that was offered, the next question would be, "Is something wrong?"

Over the years, I developed a tolerance for alcohol, and as a result, I needed more to get a good buzz. My alcohol abuse accelerated throughout my twenties and into my thirties. I told myself that quitting weed was enough because it was illegal, and with that logic, I was maintaining my values. I continued drinking because everyone was doing it, I enjoyed it, and it was all I needed.

The same routine went on weekly, month after month, year after year. I worked during the day and headed to the bar most nights to see what the guys were doing—hanging out and partying on the weekends. When not drinking with friends, I often drank alone at home. During this time, I started trying to control my drinking with little success.

I thought that alcohol was my friend. I relied on it for courage, strength, peace of mind, and survival. In reality, alcohol was my greatest enemy, cloaking itself in my emotions while violently and shamelessly manipulating me to gather strength for the next battle. Every move I made to control my drinking, no matter how much planning I put into it, would result in a stronger enemy.

Today, I understand that I used alcohol to escape reality, medicate, and numb the emotional pain. As a teenager and young adult, I constructed a heavily fortified emotional fortress within myself. I walled myself in for protection, only to realize I had allowed alcoholism inside these fortified emotional walls. I was so confident that my way would work that I believed it would allow me to continue drinking with impunity, only to discover that alcohol would repeatedly kick the crap out of me. I was trapped in my small, self-centered world.

No sane army would build a bridge so the enemy could easily access the battlefield. No sane person would lay a minefield behind them, forget where they placed the mines, and then run through them while in retreat. I did all these things and more. I repeatedly tried so many stupid, self-initiated, ridiculous, bizarre, and painful things to myself to stop drinking. I engaged in this magical thinking for many years.

I was also a great bullshit artist. From an early age, I could talk my way out of most precarious situations. On one occasion, I stayed at a ski club in a small New Hampshire town. My friend and I decided to go from one party to another because the one we were at was running low on alcohol. I'm driving along when the blue lights come on behind me. I pulled over and told her not to say anything and let me do the talking.

The officer approached my car and requested my license and registration. "Yes, sir," I replied. "No problems here, officer. Whatever you need."

I noticed him looking at my eyes and trying to smell my breath as he held the flashlight. "Have you been drinking," he asked.

I was completely hammered, but as a bullshit artist, I was ready with a convincing answer. "Well, yes, sir. I had a couple, but please let me explain. My girlfriend and I are heading back to our place. We just left a birthday party for a friend. Was I going too fast, officer?" I meekly inquired.

"Shut the engine off while I run a check," he said.

"Okay," I said, "but I must explain something before you do that. I have an interview for a job in law enforcement on Monday morning. If I get a ticket, I must explain what happened, which could set me back for a year or more."

"What kind of job are you going for," he asked.

"I passed the test and background check for the US Marshal Service. I'm in the final interview phase. I've been waiting for years for this job. It is my dream to be a US Marshal. Anything happens at this stage, and I am out," I said.

"Where is the interview," he asked.

"It's in the JFK Federal Building in Boston. Government Center on Cambridge Street."

He looked deeply at my remorseful face and said, "Okay, sit tight." Soon after, he returned to my vehicle and handed me my license and registration. "I'll give you a break this time! Slow down and go home."

I thanked him and promised I would do just that. As I drove away, the young woman in the car said she didn't know that I was going to be a US Marshal. She was so impressed.

I turned to look at her and said, "Are you nuts? I'm not joining the US Marshals. That was all BS. I didn't want to get arrested for driving under the influence."

Off to the next party!

At age thirty, I had an excellent job with a good salary. I was independent. I was successful. I had accomplished my education and career goals and owned my own home. *Life is good, or so I thought. I'm responsible for myself, and I'm doing well. I'm safe so long as I don't do hard drugs.* But man, let me tell you, there were plenty of temptations to do drugs, especially when I was drinking.

I knew I drank much more than the average person, and I tried many strategies to control my drinking. I changed drinks, changed bars, changed friends. I sipped wine when I was home alone. Sometimes, I would choose a restaurant with only a license to sell beer and wine to avoid hard liquor. I tried different drinks or would drink a glass of water between beers. An attempt at having a non-alcoholic beverage such as Coca-Cola would inevitably evolve into a rum and Coke before the night was over.

My friends also drank but to differing degrees. Friends in one group were heavy drinkers and drug users, while friends in another group were moderate drinkers. I would hang out with the group that matched my mood. I even tried drinking with friends who were social drinkers, thinking if I were around others who weren't drinking to get drunk, I wouldn't either. But ironically, being with a group of social drinkers was the most challenging for me. My compulsion to drink was ever-present, and I always wanted more.

My childhood experiences followed me into adulthood, but I had no idea how deeply they had affected me. I often felt uncomfortable, so I tried everything available to try and fix myself, except looking at my drinking. That was off-limits. I honestly believed that alcohol was beneficial and necessary to cope with day-to-day living. Alcohol was my friend and my therapist. Alcohol was not the problem, I thought. I tried to compensate by reading self-help books, attending lectures on family dysfunction, and working out excessively. I continued swimming and running, entered many 5K and 10K races and triathlons, and even earned a black belt in karate after a few years of training. Anything to prove that I did not have a drinking problem!

I had relationships with several remarkable women I loved but could not make a lifetime commitment. Relationships and commitments interfered with my drinking and made me feel I was not in control. I was unprepared to trust and feel like an adult because this meant vulnerability. Regrettably, I associated my parents' married life with a dysfunctional home—too much arguing, anger, fear, and hurt—and I wanted none of that. I pledged that my home would not be like the one I lived in as a kid. When it came to relationships, I didn't know whether I was coming or going. I always felt that if I did get married, I would be marring my future ex-wife.

Because I was active in sports and politics in the community, I always had a large group of friends and associates. We all drank excessively. We often went out "clubbing" in groups or attended various parties. We drank at organized sports events, such as basketball, hockey, and flag football. We took many vacations to Acapulco, Cape Cod, or skiing up north. For many of these vacations, we sat in the bar and partied. In many ways, my friends provided the support and connection my family did not offer. Social relationships were vital to me.

A group of guys in my neighborhood started a flag football league, and we played on Sunday mornings for many years. I enjoyed the camaraderie and friendships based more on drinking than sportsmanship. We would head to the bar for lunch after each game, and at the end of the year, we had an awards celebration with a banquet and open bar. It was worth getting up early on Sunday morning during football season to play just to be able to attend the annual open bar banquet.

Things looked great on the outside, but none of these activities filled the void in me. On the inside, I was stuck in a fearful, lonely rut. Despite having many friends and drinking buddies, I never really felt close to anyone. When I was in a room with numerous friends, I felt alone. People admired my independence, but little did they know it was solitary and lonely independence, one for which drinking seemed to offer a temporary solution. I thought that the best thing to do was push away family, friends, God, spirituality, and my health when, in fact, this is how alcoholism strengthened itself. The pain and loneliness were winning. Things were looking and feeling ominous.

For several years, I'd stop drinking for a month at a time, proudly proclaiming this amazing accomplishment, trying to impress my friends that I was in control. I mainly was trying to convince myself.

None of my strategies worked. Usually, I got wasted and promised myself that it would be different next time. It was always going to be different next time. Denial carried me through each episode and on to the next time. Or I would start to drink excessively to make up for all the drinks I had "given up" that month. My obsession and compulsion to drink were always present. I also drove under the influence of alcohol, not caring that I was putting myself and others at risk. The hangovers were relentless and getting more vicious. I continued to pledge that it would be different the next time.

In reality, I was an insecure and empty shell, continuing on while deceiving myself about my alcohol abuse. I constantly lied to myself, promising that I would change. Looking back, I now realize that I was deeply in denial about the extent and consequences of my alcohol abuse. I was trapped in my alcoholic world, filled with lies and addiction. I was functioning but not satisfactorily, trudging along miserably as my weekly hangovers worsened. I lived a life without honest self-reflection or knowledge of how to grow and thrive. I lacked a spiritual connection or beliefs. I had no understanding of what a relationship with God could be like. In my brokenness, I believed God abandoned me and may have been angry with me or punishing me for an unknown reason. I had no interest in having God in my life. This lonely and shameful existence persisted for another six years, excruciating years.

Doing the things I said I would never do.

The opportunity to do drugs was always present around the neighborhood. Prescription drugs, acid, black beauties, amphetamines, downers, uppers, hash, cocaine, and—the most feared—heroin were plentiful in the neighborhood. I drank, often alone, three or four days a week, but I promised myself not to use drugs. I still had my standards about drugs and vowed never to do any hard drugs. Never, I repeated to myself daily. Not for me! Only sleazy reprobates did hard drugs. I had gone through my marijuana phase at a younger age and barely survived. I had tried several other drugs, uppers, and downers, including mescaline and speed, but I was not too fond of their effects. Also, I had witnessed so many lives of good friends destroyed by harder drugs, which frightened me. In addition, drug use interfered with my work, and I thought their high cost was a waste of hard-earned money. I preferred alcohol to drugs and was confident that my determination and street smarts would protect me.

For years, I watched friends or associates do lines of cocaine, which seemed to go hand in hand with drinking. While inhaling the white powder through their nostrils, they proclaim, "God, this stuff is good shit. It costs more than gold." I always said it was not for me. I worked too hard for my money to waste it on cocaine. I had my standards. "No thanks," I would say when offered a line or just a taste. Dealers use the term "just a taste" to get you to sample the goods—once you have a "taste," you want more!

Following my parents' example, I was also a heavy cigarette smoker. I probably started smoking regularly at fourteen, as did most of my friends. Smoking seemed to go hand in hand with drinking. I attempted to stop smoking many, many times without success. Particularly during swim season, I would try to quit without much luck. My swim team coach caught me smoking in the boy's bathroom in high school. He walked in on a few of us guys smoking and looked at me as he ordered everyone out. As I walked by, he punched me in the stomach with a closed fist and knocked the wind out of me. I almost went down. He said I would be off the team if he saw me smoking again. That didn't stop me. In those days, you took a punch from the teacher, kept your mouth shut, and plotted how to get them back. Even watching my Mom suffer a prolonged and painful death from lung and colon cancer failed to deter me from stopping smoking cigarettes.

As a young adult, I continued drinking, smoking, and hanging out with the guys at the bar or partying around the city. (A professional courtesy of being a bartender at a popular club is that you usually do not have to pay for drinks in other clubs. When other bartenders came to my club, I took care of their drinks, and when I went to theirs, they took care of mine.)

One particular Saturday evening, I was hanging out with some friends—guys I tended bar and worked with at the clubs. I had a good buzz from all the drinking when someone said, "Let's get some coke."

"I'm not interested," I immediately replied. "That crap is not for me."

The guys moved to an open table in the corner of the room when someone said, "Grab your drinks. We're moving."

I went ahead and moved to the table and saw one of my buddies doing a line of cocaine. It looked fun, glamorous, and exciting. Once again, I was offered a "line" and declined. Then one of the guys said, "Do it, man. You can drink all night!" At this stage in my life, I thought I was drinking plenty. I did not need a chemical to increase my endurance. But he persisted, "No, you can stay up longer and drink more."

I was adamant about not doing a line when another guy said, "It's unbelievable shit. Go ahead, try some."

And just like that, I did a line of cocaine.

He took a rolled-up hundred-dollar bill and handed it to me. For some reason, everyone seemed to enjoy the cocaine better out of a hundred-dollar bill. Supposedly, those bills travel through fewer hands and are cleaner, which is presumed to enhance the effect. I couldn't care less where it was from. I pushed the rolled-up bill into my nose and snorted the white powder into my sinus cavity. At first, it burned and was a little painful. But the very next thing I knew, I felt euphoric. *Wow! Where have you been all my life?*

Five minutes later, I was asking for more! Five minutes after that, I was demanding more! *Give me more! I can take on the whole world now.* I did not make it home until 3:30 a.m., stumbling into my house, drunk and high from alcohol and cocaine, hammered and feeling ill. The next day, I woke up physically sick with a savage hangover and blocked sinuses. I had done something I said I would never do, something I loathed. Full of shame and remorse, I swore to God I would never do that again. *What happened to me? How did I do the drugs I promised myself I would never do? I will not do that again. Never,* I pledged to myself.

Two weeks later, I was drinking, smoking, and having a good time with the same group when someone said, "Let's do some lines." My immediate reaction was, *No way! I am not interested in doing any cocaine tonight or ever again, for that matter.*

I sipped my drink from a distance and watched as a couple of guys did their lines. The night went on, as did the shots of tequila.

I had a good buzz when one of my friends said, "Do you want a taste? You'll be able to stay up and party."

I gave in, honestly believing that I would do only one line. Ten minutes later, I was asking—no, demanding—more cocaine. The next day, I woke up with a throbbing, painful hangover and, once again, felt remorse and shame for doing something I had pledged not to do. *I did it again*, I thought. My resilience, determination, and street smarts—the very assets that had carried me this far in life—were useless. Saying no to alcohol and drugs was futile. I could not overcome the enticement.

This scenario repeated itself many times. I insisted that I was not interested in doing cocaine—until I gave in. Unfortunately, once I started drinking alcohol, cocaine became part of my routine. Wasn't I going to be different than those other guys? I ended my nights and mornings thinking *I would control my drinking to avoid using cocaine. I will be different!* Yet, I did it again and again. I was living in denial, believing my lies.

My tolerance for alcohol and cocaine continued to increase. I was steadfast in my desire and determination not to do it again, but my emotions were a train wreck. The guilt, shame, and remorse were painful emotional albatrosses around my neck. But I was too proud and too fearful to ask for help. *Only wimps and weaklings ask for help*, I thought. *I am a confident, independent, resilient kid from the project.* I tried to convince myself that I could handle this. In reality, I was becoming increasingly desperate, feeling as if there was a dark cloud over my head. My life was getting worse day by day. I had a big problem I thought nobody could understand. I was alone.

The Last Night Out

By the grace of God, my last drink was on Sunday, October 7, 1990. I was not planning on drinking that day. I was determined not to drink that day because I was still hurting from drinking and using cocaine the previous weekend and constantly running out of money. I was finally looking forward to a quiet and comfortable night at home.

I planned to enjoy a relaxing evening with a recently purchased paperback book and a mug of hot tea. On Saturday afternoon, with my tea mug and book ready, I remembered there was a building and construction material trade show at a nearby convention center. I decided to go there late in the afternoon before returning home to read and relax. As I left my house, I pledged that I would only have a ginger ale if offered the opportunity to drink. That night would be different because I was not drinking.

I arrived at the trade show around four. I proceeded up and down the aisles, enjoying the displays of the appliances, cabinets, and other building materials. While browsing, I came across a friend, Janet, working at one of the displays. I had partied with Janet many times before, and I was fond of her, mainly because she sold cocaine and had "cuffed" or extended credit to me many times. She was also good for a "little taste" of cocaine now and then.

We started chatting, and I was extra nice because I had an ulterior motive: I didn't intend to drink or use any cocaine that evening, but I was laying the groundwork for future nights of partying, putting some "goodwill" in the bank. I was a good listener and agreed with everything she said. Looking back, I wish I had dedicated this much effort to something more productive.

She told me she would get off work at six and would love to grab a drink. I told her I wasn't drinking but would hang out with her in the lounge. I was not planning on doing any lines of cocaine either that night. I pledged to myself again that I would order a ginger ale. Honestly, a single ginger ale.

We met in the lounge at six o'clock and sat at the bar. The bartender asked what we were having. I repeated to myself, *just order ginger ale. Stick with the ginger ale.* Janet ordered a screwdriver, and the bartender turned to me. I was thinking ginger ale, but when my mouth opened, I heard, "I'll have what she's having, but make mine with the top-shelf vodka." I thought to myself, *Where the fuck did that come from? What about the ginger ale?*

I sat at the bar with a perfect poker face, yet confusion and shock swirled within me. I had rehearsed my drink order in my head over and over for almost an hour while I waited for my friend to get off work. *Stay with the ginger ale,* I had said to myself. This night would be like many nights I had had over the last six years. I had lost count of how often I said, "*I did it again.*" Just like I did the previous weekends.

I had no idea what I was up against or how little control I had over my alcoholism and drug use. I didn't want to drink that evening, and I certainly didn't want to use drugs. Absolutely, no drugs, I proclaimed! My previous experiences had shown me that drugs took me to the wrong places with the wrong people, where I made regrettable decisions. But something different was going on with my emotions. I was powerless to control my drinking, realizing this had become my pattern over the years.

In the blink of an eye, I shrug off the moment of clarity and return to the conversation as though nothing had happened. We engaged in what seemed like a beautiful conversation and laughed. After two drinks, Janet whispers, "How about a line?"

"I thought you would never ask," I said. I followed her into the women's room, ensuring we were not being watched, and locked the door as we proceeded to do our first line of cocaine for the evening.

We returned to the lounge and finished our drinks as we talked about the remainder of the evening. The lounge closes at nine, and we need a plan afterward. I think about a club I know will be crowded and loud. "Let's go to Quincy," I say. She agrees to go. I also invited the bartender, Nancy, who decided she'd meet us there.

"Before heading to Quincy, let's buy some more cocaine," I say. Janet is running low, and I want to show that I am a "stand-up guy" and will get some cocaine to share with her. I'm showing off.

Shortly after nine, I drive to my regular dealer's house for an "8 Ball" of cocaine, or an eighth of an ounce, which is about 3.5 grams and costs about three hundred dollars. During this period in my life, I had several dealers on speed dial. I ran into his house to make the purchase and sampled the goods as Janet waited in the car.

About now, I have an excellent cocaine buzz going. I'm high as I tell my dealer to break up the cocaine into grams for packaging, so I'd have some for tomorrow. The truth is that I don't want to share more than one gram with my friend. I return to the car. I lied to Janet by telling her that my dealer only had one gram. I kept the remainder hidden in my pocket.

We leave, and once again, I am hammered, driving recklessly across the city to the nightclub in Quincy. I'm a liar, a cheat, and a thief, but I don't care. I feel exhilarated and on top of my game! I think I'm fooling everyone. We do a line of coke in the car before going into the bar and ordering drinks. I'm having a blast, and we are dancing and singing with the band. *This is a wicked pissah time! I am the man! I'm with a good-looking girl, buying drinks for strangers and doing lines of cocaine when nobody is looking.* The bartender, Nancy, is there now and is also having a blast! *Life is good*, I think.

As the night goes on, I do some of Janet's cocaine and then head to the men's room alone to use more from my hidden pocket stash. Then, back to the bar for another drink. When I hear someone say, "Last call," I think, *What?* I'm not ready for the last call. It's one in the morning, and I am just getting started. I want more action, more excitement.

I tell Janet and Nancy I know of an after-hours club open all night in South Boston in an old warehouse. I have no idea how I am able to drive. Off we go, continuing our drinking and drugging at the after-hours party. I stay until five-thirty before I leave Janet and Nancy behind, stumbling out the door, jumping into my car, and driving the four blocks home.

I have no idea how I will make it home safely. When I arrived home, I was sick to my stomach and throwing up all over the place. I tried to take an aspirin to stop my throbbing head, but I vomited that up.

I lay on the bed face down, desperately wanting it to stop. I want to die to stop the pain. The sun is coming up, and daylight is entering through the windows. I am too drunk to get up and too high from the cocaine to pass out. This madness must stop now. I think about grabbing my gun and blowing my brains out. It seems like my only option. I start to cry. I am alone, sick, confused, and miserable.

I'd just spent five hundred dollars that night when I'd told myself I only wanted ginger ale. Once again, I'm drinking and using drugs without my own permission. A total loss of control over alcohol. I am overcome with shame because "I did it again." I say to myself, *Get up and grab your gun and end this bullshit.* I want to die. I ask God to take me now and stop all this insanity.

Frightened and confused, I am at the lowest point in my life. No childhood experience was as detrimental to my psyche as this one was. I have done this to myself. My control, independence, determination, and resilience are all a deception—a big fat lie. My current situation is, apparently, the best I can do. This—wanting to die—is as good as it gets for me with alcohol and drugs. My best thinking has brought me to this point. I cannot blame my father for this predicament. This is on me and my behavior. All the enjoyment from drinking and using drugs has disappeared. My alcohol and drug use has escalated beyond anything I could have imagined. *This is not me,* I thought. *I didn't sign up for this. It's dreadful in every conceivable way.*

I continued to have the dry heaves and decided to get a sip of water to get the taste of vomit out of my mouth. As I walk past the mirror above my dresser, I loathe the sight of myself. *Nothing but a drunk and drug-addicted loser,* I think. I go downstairs to the kitchen, telling myself, *"You fuckin' suck,"* under my breath. Walking past the kitchen table, I see my paperback book and the mug with the teabag I intended to have yesterday. All of my good intentions flood my mind. I say to myself, "You did it again." I feel disgusted with myself and utterly humiliated. In all the times of catching a good buzz and getting high, I have never felt more disgusted with myself. I tried to sip a little water, only to gag. Dazed and confused, I stumble back to my bedroom. I keep telling myself to end this madness, asking myself, *What the fuck happened?*

Not only am I disgusted at myself, depressed, alone, full of self-loathing, embarrassed, and humiliated, but physically sick. I am starting to believe that suicide is a credible option and that there is no way out of this darkness. I'd acquired a handgun when I was a summer cop, and it is nearby in my bedroom closet.

"Do it," I say to myself. "You're a pussy. You got no balls—do it."

I hit my emotional bottom and believe there is no way out of this darkness. After a few more hours of this horrible feeling, I finally quieted my mind long enough to get a couple of hours of sleep. I wake with the worst, most vicious, brutal hangover ever. Once again, I feel the physical effect of the last evening and everything I have been chasing with alcohol and drugs for the previous six years and beyond. My head and sinuses are throbbing, my eyes are bloodshot, and my nostrils are blocked with cocaine residue.

I am angry all over again, asking myself what happened. *How could I let myself go this way? What the fuck is wrong with me?* Physically, I feel horrible, shaking, and sick to my stomach. The condition I am in—the situation I put myself in—is harsh and unforgiving. I went to have ginger ale and spent five hundred dollars on alcohol and drugs. Emotionally, I am at the lowest, darkest point in my life. Nothing has ever happened to me that is more emotionally debilitating than this. Later, I learned that people in recovery describe this state as being visited by the "hideous four horsemen: terror, bewilderment, frustration, and despair." That day, each of them visited me and left their mark.

Less than ten hours before, I had felt like I was on top of the world, but now despair engulfs me. Baffled and anguished, I have no idea what to do next. I want it all to stop. I want to feel normal. I want to be free of all the emotional pain that is part of me.

I do not have many options. I cannot kill myself, although that was my first option. Am I sick and desperate enough to ask for help? Can I manage to live through this day? Was this my "bottom?" *God, I hope so. I can't do this again,* I think to myself. *I would rather die than relive this day.* I am a broken man physically, emotionally, and spiritually. Because of my addiction, I have exiled myself from hope and humanity. I'm experiencing confusion and deep despair. I'm devoid of all hope and cannot even fathom its possibility. I desperately need some hope to survive. How dark it is before the light.

PART II

Washed Ashore: There is Help

The next day, I decided to call a friend, Patrick. He was a member of a self-help recovery group in South Boston. They were known to meet in church basements, which didn't impress me as I had not been inside a church in years. It was not an easy decision, but I knew I had to make this call. I thought I had a good run, but this lifestyle was killing me.

Fear and shame blocked my ability to think clearly, but I was desperate and had to do something. Two of my older brothers were members of a similar recovery group, and I was too embarrassed to reach out to them. As ridiculous as it sounds, I didn't want them to think that I had a problem with alcohol. I didn't want them to believe that I was like our Dad. Continuing this painful merry-go-round was no longer an option. I knew that I could not go on this way. I was sure that the drugs and alcohol were going to kill me. Understanding and accepting this fact allowed me to change my life and end my battle with alcohol and drugs one day at a time.

I called Patrick, and my hands were trembling. When he answered, I almost hung up. I felt so ashamed. But I had had enough. I was sick of my life and had to ask for help.

The conversation began with the usual "How ya doing? What's up?" But when Patrick asked what was up with me, I froze. After a long pause, I asked him if he still went to "those meetings."

He stated that he did go and wondered why I was asking.

"I think I want to check it out," I said.

"That's great! I'm going tonight. Why don't you join me."

I was so afraid that someone from my neighborhood would see me coming out of a church basement filled with recovering alcoholics that I insisted we find a meeting miles away from South Boston. Patrick agreed, and we went to a recovery meeting on the other side of town that evening.

I didn't know what to expect and was frightened walking into the meeting. I was consumed with self-centered fear. I listened to all the speakers as best I could, but mostly, I didn't understand what was said. I was spiritually bankrupt—nothing but an empty shell. I had become the alcoholic my father was, and I despised myself. I was a hypocrite and a fraud, and I wanted to die. My friends and acquaintances often described me as one of the good guys, someone you could count on if you needed a favor, just like people had said of my Dad. Inside, I felt like anything but that.

That night, I recall hearing something about "joining a group, getting a sponsor, and asking for help." But the most hopeful and powerful statement I heard was, "I would never have to experience my last night of drinking again,"—which amazed me. I would not have wished my last night on my worst enemy. I knew I could not survive another night like that, a night of darkness and despair with an overwhelming feeling of no way out.

My journey to recovery started that day. By the grace of God, my last drink was early in the morning on Sunday, October 7, 1990. This sounds improbable, but it was both the darkest day of my life and the best day.

The first year of recovery

When my recovery began, I was thirty-six years old, and I am grateful that I started this path when I did. Although the road to sobriety was lengthy and, at times, agonizing, I consider myself lucky. My determination kicked in when I decided to get sober and did what I had to do. I vowed to go to meetings and seek a solution for my problem with alcohol. Previous experience had taught me that my profound and sincere determination not to drink alcohol was useless. I realized that I couldn't get sober on my own, but I could succeed with the support of others who have had similar experiences.

At first, I struggled to fully commit to the recovery program because I was highly guarded and believed I needed to control my environment. For years, I had told people I was handling my drinking. The occasional blackout was an anomaly I could easily dismiss with some flimsy excuse. *Hadn't I practically raised myself, paid for college and a nice car, and purchased my own home? I accomplished this because of my grit, resilience, and perseverance. I could manage my life just fine, thank you very much!*

I had repeatedly said this to myself, believing it was true. I always thought I could stop drinking at any time, but I had tried to stop so many times that I had lost count. In reality, I was powerless over alcohol, and my drinking was out of control.

I have friends raised in a similar trauma-filled environment who do not have a problem with substance abuse; they have good lives, and I am happy for them. But many of my drinking friends, ones I grew up with or met along the way, are still actively drinking. Many have severe alcohol and drug problems, cannot hold a job, have broken families, and live chaotic lives. Several became homeless, incarcerated, or died. A few still live in the public housing project.

That October night, I realized that I needed to change or perish. When I discovered sobriety, there was both good news and bad news. The good news was that the battle was over, but the bad news was that not only had I lost the war against alcohol, but I was my own enemy. If I had not found my way into a recovery program, I would have continued down a destructive path of pain and suffering, trapped in a chaotic life of alcohol abuse. My life would have been unproductive and devoid of meaning. I was headed towards incarceration, institutions, or even death.

Throughout the recovery process, each step taught me something valuable. I understood that I couldn't control other people and that they would never do what I wanted when I wanted. I wish I had known this as a kid because it would have saved me a lot of heartache and misery.

Many people talked about their group, a sponsor, a spiritual being somewhere "out there," or God as their "Higher Power." But when someone mentioned God, I shut down and became indifferent. Frankly, as I've said, I wanted nothing to do with God. God abandoned me as a kid, left me in that emotionally complicated and terrifying house in the project, and took my mother away too early. If anything, I believed he was a punishing God, and I was on his hit list! I let God know that I had kicked him out of my life the day I decided to no longer kiss my Dad good night at bedtime. My traumatic childhood experiences taught me that trusting anyone would only result in emotional pain. I wanted a spiritual relationship but had been burned too many times. I would not let myself be disappointed again by placing my spiritual care into the hand of God. I was sure that the results would be the same. The pain and the fear were too great to risk. That would be nothing more than a setup for loneliness, misery, and regret. Just what did God have to do with my drinking and drugging anyway? I didn't see the connection or the necessity of having God in my life. If this was the direction of the recovery group, then maybe I should head to the door. I felt this recovery program did not understand and could not help me.

Fortunately, members of the recovery group were exceedingly kind and patient. I shared that the God part of the recovery program was not for me at one meeting. I informed some group members that I had a problem with God. "So, I'll ignore the God part of the message," I told them. A couple of people smiled, and a few smirked. Most just nodded their heads in agreement. I concluded that this meant they understood the way I was feeling. Many said, "Just keep coming, Tim. We need you! Choosing your own concept of a "higher power" is all that matters."

Charlie and My First Group

When I first joined a recovery group in my neighborhood, at the urging of my good friend Jack, I was very apprehensive. I did not know the expectations for new group members, but I dived in anyway. I approached the group secretary. "Hi, I'm new and would like to join this group," I said.

The secretary looked at me with a broad smile and said, "Great!" He asked my name and then said, "Welcome, Tim! I'll put you on the list along with the other members. You may use the list to contact another member if you wish. It's confidential, so we only use first names and the first letter of your last name."

"What else do you need from me?" I was expecting a request for dues or being a driver or something!

"Nothing, just come to the meeting each week. We can always use some help setting up the hall or making coffee. It's a great way to meet the other members of our group. If you like, you can come with the other members on commitments. New members don't share at meetings unless they have 90 days of sobriety." "Just come along for the ride," he said.

"Oh, and one more thing." "Now that you're a group member, I have a suggestion. Never miss your home group meeting. Never," he said, once again with a smile!

During a cigarette and coffee break halfway through the meeting, several group members introduced themselves and welcomed me. They could not have been more pleasant and inviting. They tried their best to put this reluctant and reticent person at ease. I'm sure it was apparent that I was full of fear and not ready to let my guard down, that I was scanning the room for a quick exit if necessary. That was just me being hyper-vigilant, a skill I learned in childhood.

One man approached me, introduced himself as Charlie, and said he was also from Southie. I knew who he was because he was a "biker" with a reputation in the neighborhood as someone not to be trusted. I also knew he had spent time in state prison for various crimes. He was not my cup of tea if you know what I mean. I gave him the cold shoulder, cut him short, and made an excuse to get away from him. *I'm better than that*, I thought.

When the meeting opened for the second half, Charlie was the speaker. My reaction was that I had nothing in common with him, and I did not want anything to do with this guy. *He's a freakin' loser,* I thought. I was stuck in the middle of the row next to my buddy Jack and could not quickly get out without being obvious. So, I sat and listened to the former inmate, Charlie. *Here we go,* I thought. *This is going to be a waste of my valuable time.* Charlie introduced himself to the crowd as a recovering alcoholic. Jack turned to me, saying, "Try to identify with this speaker, Tim."

My sarcastic reply was, "I didn't do any time in the big house, Jack!" I doubted Charlie and I had anything in common. Jack just smiled and turned his head to focus on the speaker.

Charlie started sharing the story of his checkered criminal history and substance abuse and didn't leave out any incidents that others would consider embarrassing or humiliating. He took responsibility for his behavior and the acts that had landed him in jail. He shared these experiences with humility and grace. That floored me because I had expected to get a sugar-coated version of "I'm innocent" or "Poor me. I was framed." But no! He was authentic and spoke the unabashed truth. I was transfixed and could not take my eyes off him. He gave this talk with a sense of humor, too. Everyone was laughing as he shared his message of hope and recovery. I had never heard a person talk about how they had taken drugs and had made poor choices that had landed them in prison, who could laugh at their insanity.

His talk was spellbinding. I had never heard anyone speak like this guy. It was not about his crimes but the fact he was sharing! I thought: *This guy is putting it all out there for everyone to hear and telling us that his life has improved since he got sober. I respect anyone that would do what he just did.* Charlie looked directly at me and said, "My life gets infinitesimally better every day if I stay away from a drink and a drug." *What?* I thought. *What the heck is that? Why the heck are you looking at me?*

He continued talking about what this recovery group meant to him, saying something very appealing to me. "Walking into these halls was like someone placed a warm blanket on me and welcomed me home. Home. A warm, loving, and caring home where I'm safe and taken care of." *Does that even exist? If it does, then I want that too,* I thought.

After the meeting, Charlie walked up to me, put his hand out, looked at me intently, and said, "Tim, it was nice to see you at the meeting tonight. I hope that you come back next week." I didn't say it to him, but I wanted whatever this guy had.

After a few weeks of regularly attending this meeting, Charlie invited me to join him and several other members on a "commitment" to a public shelter where we would conduct a recovery meeting. My self-centered fear kicked in at times like this, leading to harsh judgment. Initially, my first reaction was, "No thanks. I have something to do next Saturday." This was a lie because I had nothing to do on Saturday. I had never entered a public shelter and didn't have any desire to go. Not only that, but

I also didn't want to get into a car with this former inmate. I judged this man and quickly concluded he had nothing valuable to offer me.

He tried again. "Join us, Tim. It's a lot of fun, and you'll get to know some group members. The ride over and back is always a blast! I think your friend Jack will be joining us."

I told him I did not have enough time in the program to speak, so I would take a pass.

With a big smile, he said, "That's okay. You don't have to speak. You can sit with our group and be a power of example to a newcomer. Some new persons will see you in the meeting, getting sober, and think, if he can do it, then I could do it. Just come along for the ride."

I relented because I didn't have anything to do on Saturday. For the next few weeks, I went with Charlie and several other group members to a public detox and homeless shelter to convey the message of hope. I had thought I would never be caught dead in these places! I started to get comfortable around the people in my group because they knew how to stay sober and be happy. More importantly, I was staying sober.

As the years passed, Charlie became my friend, and my admiration and respect for him grew immensely. I sought him out when I had doubts about my sobriety or struggled with my alcoholic identity, which frequently occurred during the first few years of recovery. He never judged me but would tell me of his experiences when he was new and what steps he had taken. He always assured me that I was a good man, that what I felt was to be expected, and that things would get better if "you just don't drink." He was always willing to help a newcomer to the group.

Charlie generously used his money to create sober housing for people transitioning out of prison. He selflessly dedicated his time as a volunteer at homeless shelters and food pantries. He tirelessly advocated for changing the laws so that individuals who had successfully transformed their lives wouldn't face employment barriers due to their past criminal records. Years later, he volunteered as a facilitator for recovery meetings at the jail where I worked. Typically, former felons were not allowed in the County Jail, but Charlie was an exception. He did such an excellent job that the Sheriff requested that Charlie expand the groups to the House of Corrections.

Charlie's hand was always there for another alcoholic. He would say, "I don't care if you're from Jail or Yale—you can stay sober, and we have the solution." He was also one of the people that offered to me: "Let us love you until you can love yourself." He must have known I was down in the dumps and didn't love myself when he said those comforting words. I am so grateful!

After that first night, each time Charlie would see me at the meeting, he would make it a point to walk over to me and welcome me. He always smiled and had a positive attitude and confidence in the recovery program he wanted to share with everyone. He could see my fear and awkward attempts to keep some distance, but he never gave up carrying the message of hope. Whenever I was down, he would remind me that my life would get "infinitesimally" better each day if I didn't drink that day. That's only a tiny amount, but it's going in the right direction and improves daily. He was a better man than me. His power of example, charisma, and confidence assured me everything would be okay. I often thought that if this guy could stay sober, so could I. Looking back, I can say without any doubt that Charlie was right.

Meeting Charlie was one of my high points in becoming sober, and I was grateful for his friendship. This man, who had nothing in common with me, taught me by example with humility, kindness, service to others, and how to stay sober one day at a time. He helped save my life. It must have been the grace of God that put people like Charlie in my life. It was no longer just me fighting this alcohol problem; now, we were. I am part of the group now and so grateful for the many recovering men and women who showed me how to live substance-free.

The people I met in recovery possessed a sense of centeredness and were grounded and in union with something greater than themselves. They displayed qualities of maturity, joyfulness, honesty, and patience that I found inspiring and contagious. Although I could not pinpoint the source of these attributes at the time, I now recognize it as hope. I understood that to change, I had to be open to new relationships and continuously strive to improve them. Whenever I met a spiritual person, I instinctively recognized their unique qualities, free from unhealthy fears and resentments. Unhealthy fears and bitterness were not guiding them. I needed to remain open to new relationships, both with others and with myself, for internal change to occur and allow the positive character traits of loving, happy, and sober individuals to rub off on me and promote hope. The most rewarding aspect was becoming a reflection of these positive and sober experiences.

I believe the empathy I received and the authenticity and humility I witnessed in the recovery groups opened my eyes to a new way of seeing myself. Their unconditional positive regard for me was internalized and renewed my sense of self. I started to change and perceive myself in a more hopeful way. I was no longer motivated and driven by self-centered fear and uncertainty about my identity; I felt understood and accepted without judgment.

Before my sobriety, I often reflected on the negative consequences of my childhood and adulthood experiences, which were detrimental, unhealthy, and depressing. However, in these meetings, I encountered something strange. By listening to people share their experiences, I discovered things about myself by relating to them. I heard how others felt and acted just like me and that I was not alone in my thinking and feelings. These were people from similar backgrounds and individuals from seemingly perfect homes with loving parents and safe environments. Yet, they, too, struggled with alcoholism and lost control over their drinking. Despite their idyllic backgrounds, they were just like me. Other people described families that sounded exactly like those on the family shows I watched on TV as a kid. They had things I thought would have given me a better life. Their dad was not terrorizing the family, so I figured their lives must be perfect.

These people who had grown up in well-off suburbs with two cars and family vacations sat beside me in the meetings because they also couldn't stop drinking and lost control over alcohol. Remarkably, they also had similar fears and insecurities and drank like me. Many others came from dysfunctional homes, but they learned how to stay sober and offered to help me. I could identify with them and feel their pain as I felt my emotions. Realizing that others think, feel, and act just like me was a revelation. They possessed the same feelings and unpleasant emotions as mine, and many intentionally medicated themselves with alcohol and drugs as I did.

Slowly, each day, I began changing for the better because I was in recovery and began discovering my true self. There was hope for me in this recovery program. People were genuine when they urged me to keep coming and said, "We need you." The thought that they needed me boosted my self-esteem. It soothed my troubled soul when a person I didn't know intimately said, "Let us love you until you can love yourself."

Eventually, although reluctantly, I became a more active participant. Some group members asked me to stand at the front door and be the greeter. My initial reaction was stern, "No! I'm not doing that!" But a week later, I reconsidered. After all, these people were not drinking or doing drugs—and this was something I wanted for myself, so perhaps I should follow their suggestions. I felt accepted in the recovery group and became much more comfortable. I continued attending the meetings and became the official group greeter.

One evening at a recovery meeting, a woman asked, "Tim, why don't you install a window in the concrete tower you live in? Let in some sunshine in, maybe talk to a neighbor." It was a wake-up call because, once again, I learned that I was not alone. Others have been in the same mental trap, and they understood without judging me. At another meeting, this woman sat beside me to ask how I was doing. When I told her I was fine and happy, she smiled and said, "Then you might want to tell your face!" I needed to lighten up, be happy, and show it. These messages, delivered with love, reminded me not to take myself so seriously. I appreciated people like her.

Occasionally, someone would relapse and start drinking again. The members' reaction was remarkable because they never judged or criticized but welcomed them back with love and acceptance. There was no shame or teasing of an individual who relapsed. None of the sarcasm I had learned growing up was ever directed at such a person. I never heard anyone joke about relapse because each person could recall their painful struggles and consequences. Nobody willingly returns to a pit of despair and humiliation. There was a feeling of "There but for the grace of God go I." Members focused on the returning member with gratitude and relief that they had returned because they know that some people who relapse never get sober again.

At about this time in my recovery journey, I learned about the disease of alcoholism. Alcoholism was described as a disease of the body, mind, and spirit. When an alcoholic takes a drink, the usual reaction is to have another. A total loss of control over alcohol was something I immediately identified with. The compulsion to drink again was strong in some people but not others. Some guy described their favorite drink as "the next one." I knew exactly what that was because that was how I drank—always looking for the next one. I had lost control over my ability to refuse a drink, even when I didn't want one.

The description of an alcoholic's mind also resonated with me. I had tried to control my drinking using willpower and self-knowledge without any success. My false idea about handling my drinking repeatedly resulted in me shamefully recognizing that "I did it again." I began to realize that the control I thought I had was a blatant lie, and I was sick, angry, and disgusted from hearing myself say it.

I started feeling good about my sobriety when I heard a speaker say, "Getting sober is an inside job." *An inside job? What does that mean?* My emotions were a train wreck, scattered and broken into thousands of pieces. I didn't feel, talk about, or acknowledge my emotions. I was detached and stoic regarding emotional things and described my spirituality as nonexistent.

When the people in my recovery group described spiritual sickness, I instinctively knew this would take much work. I had no spirituality, no relationship with God. All these aspects of the disease of alcoholism were explained to me as the "inside" work I needed to do.

The situation was like that with my Dad when I was a kid. I wanted a relationship with my Dad, while at the same time, I did not. I feared the intoxicated Dad who would appear even at the best of times and ruin everything. Similarly, I craved a spiritual connection, and more importantly, I wanted to stay sober, but I also wanted to stay in control. Would I close the door and run from recovery because I was not in control? Although confusion, doubt, and self-centered fear were always prominent early in my recovery, I attended weekly recovery meetings because of the hope, love, truthfulness, and patience I witnessed in these meetings. Also, I was not confident that I could stay sober alone; therefore, I had to take a risk with these recovery people.

One woman approached me and asked, "Could you believe that I believe?" *Can I believe that she believes?* I pondered that question because it was a curious concept. I assumed she was kind to me and didn't want me to offend her or challenge her relationship with God, so I said, "Yes, I can believe that you believe." It felt like I was placing a bet on a football game using someone else's money! More importantly, I was less likely to be disappointed because I had no skin in the game. She was sober, so something was working for her, and she was entitled to her spiritual beliefs. Strangely enough, I was attracted to spiritual people and their demeanor. Their qualities and intentions were evident to me. The feeling of kindness and compassion that spiritual people tend to have and are willing to share with others is something I desired—but I wanted it without a God.

I knew enough to associate with the type of people who would make me a better person, and I believed that sober spiritual people were the ones who could do that. I felt a kindred understanding of suffering from these spiritual people in recovery. We had traveled the same path of obsession and compulsion in our alcohol abuse. In this recovery program, the sober spiritual type individuals I met knew of a way out from a dark place that had no way out.

I would sit and observe what was taking place in the meetings. I recognized people from my neighborhood who drank like me but were now sober. I watched others help a newcomer and observed that person transform into a much happier individual. They not only looked better, but many could hold their heads up and look you in the eye. They became active participants in their recovery process. They lost the shame and remorse I was still holding on to. It was a miraculous experience to witness people return to their lives, careers, and families. Something was happening there, and I wanted to be part of it. Their inside work was showing up in their outside lives. But I still needed the courage to look inside myself and do the work.

Many became more honest in their lives and would speak from the podium about the improvements that were taking place. The peace of mind they were experiencing, and their sobriety were sights to be seen. I recall watching a guy from the neighborhood, a guy I hadn't thought very highly of, receiving a medallion for five years of sobriety. I was looking at him and saying to myself, "That scumbag can't be sober," but he was. The last time I saw him, he was in the housing project selling drugs, stealing stereos, and ripping people off. He had completely turned his life around and was now a changed person. It was just amazing! When I asked my friend Jack about this, he said he believed God works through others. I still had my doubts.

Jump in—the water's great!

"And now we will hear from Tim, the newest member of our group."

As soon as my name was called, my heart started racing so rapidly that I thought it might burst out of my chest. I'd only been sober for a short six months. I attended commitments with my group members, but only as an observer. I was a passive bystander, not wanting to draw attention to myself. I knew it would eventually be my turn to share my story with strangers. The thought of speaking to a large audience was frightening because I had never spoken to any large group before.

However, the time had come, and I had agreed to speak at this open recovery meeting. My friend Jack had urged me, saying, "Don't be a taker, Tim. We must give back and carry the message of recovery." Reluctantly, I made my way to the meeting, which happened to be in my neighborhood, an area I often called "the crime scene." It was the last place I wanted to discuss my struggles with addiction publicly. I was anxious that someone in the room might recognize me from my past, or worse, be someone I had previously had a run-in with, owed money to or fought with. *What if someone knows my family?* My mind raced as I prepared a plan of escape or a flimsy excuse to avoid speaking that night. The location of exit doors became my primary concern, and it wasn't in the event of a fire in the building.

I feel as though the eyes of every person in that church basement were focused on me, including whatever spirits resided there. At this time in my recovery, I have little interest in God. It's best to leave him out of my talk tonight because he has the home-field advantage, after all. I sat there amongst the other group members, waiting for my turn to be called. I have prearranged with the chairperson, Charlie (yes, the same Charlie from my group), to be called last, hoping that time will run out so that I would not have to stand before this crowd and talk about my experiences and nascent sobriety. Much to my chagrin, I'm called first to speak by a happy and beaming recovering alcoholic! As I pass by Charlie, I lean over and whisper the exact words I uttered as a kid when things weren't going my way.

"I'm going to freakin' kill you when we get outside. I have a shank," I said with a smile.

He smiled back at me and said, "Great! Share your experience, strength, and hope, Tim. Just let God direct your words. You'll be terrific!"

Standing before a sizable crowd of fifty or sixty strangers and unaccustomed to public speaking, I have no idea what I will say. I attempt to dry my sweaty hands on my pants. I experienced tunnel vision, yet I could see various blue and gold banners around the room. The banners hanging from the walls around the room are as prominent and bright as neon signs as they project the message: "Easy does it." "One day at a time." "Let go and let God." "Progress, not perfection." And the easiest to comprehend: "Keep it simple, stupid!" That last one I can handle.

Looking over at a sea of smiling faces focused on me, I only feel fear and worry. *Will I sound stupid? What if I don't appear organized? What will people think about me? What if I forget my story? This is going to be embarrassing,* I guess. My heart continues racing, my forehead and palms sweat, and I say it. I say those words I fought for so long. These are the words that, on this day, will make me indistinguishable from my Dad. These are the exact words that I vowed never to say. Here goes nothing! My lips are quivering, and that painful lump in my throat I had as a kid returns, and I meekly say, "Hi, I'm Tim, and I'm an alcoholic!" *Here comes the fallout! Wait for it,* I thought. But nothing awful happens.

The reply is lively and welcoming, "Hi Tim!"

Jesus!! The entire room responds and says my name. Then the room goes silent as all eyes continue focusing on this speaker. I know I am speaking because several people in the front row nod slowly up and down in agreement or approval. I'm unsure, but I consider it a positive affirmation of whatever I say. It is an emotional experience, and I almost cry because I feel something positive happening. The room is silent as I share the gruesome and shameful details of the last night I went out and drank, used drugs, and wanted to blow my brains out. I explain my feelings of absolute powerlessness over alcohol and the unmanageability of my life. I proclaim that my life is getting better, a day at a time, because I am sober. Honestly, I do not recall the exact details of what I said. But I know I am in the right place with the right people. I finally take a risk, let my guard down, and trust these people to guide and care for me.

As I step down from the podium and walk back to my seat, several strangers put their hands out and say, "Great to hear you...Good message, Tim! Thank you." *Thank you.* I th*ink. I didn't do anything but scare the be-Jesus out of myself.* The two people behind me tap my shoulder and say, "Good to hear you." *I don't know what the hell I just said!*

The kindness and compassion these strangers showed me was something I was unfamiliar with, but I wanted and needed more. I was touched after the meeting when several more people walked up to me and said, "Good to hear you, and keep coming." No one was judging me! Curtie, who lived in the neighborhood and knew my family, was a man I would have regarded as having a slight drinking problem. He pulled me aside as he said, "You hit it out of the ballpark tonight. I could identify with your message. I drank and felt just like you did. Keep coming. We need you," he said. Curtie was another person I had come to admire because of his kindness and willingness to go the extra mile to help another alcoholic.

After that evening, I felt that I belonged and was accepted. *I'm going to be okay*, I thought. Charlie explained that he called me first so I wouldn't have to sit in mental anguish for 50 minutes worrying about what I would say. "You did good, kid. Keep coming," he said.

Choose Your Concept of God

Early in my sobriety, an old-timer who had been in recovery for many years told me I could choose my concept of God and decide who God was for me. He said, "Why don't you think about that and then write down all the qualities and values your ideal God would have? What do you want God to be? Define your concept of a loving God. It's your choice. You can do this." This idea floored me. The idea that I could *decide* what qualities I wanted in my God was liberating and intriguing. So I asked him what he meant.

He explained that his God, or Higher Power, was kind, loving, and always forgiving, emphasizing the word forgiving. "Meek and humble," he added. He said his Higher Power would forgive him if he were honest, humble, and tried to do the next right thing.

This concept differed from the punishing, deal-making God I had avoided all my life or the "Jail House Jesus" that people bargained with only in times of desperation.

This old-timer said he handed all his problems to God to figure out and resolve. "It is so freeing," he said. "You should try turning your will and life over to the care of God as you understand him. It also keeps me sober because I'm not preoccupied with trying to control things I can't control."

I listened attentively. I desperately wanted to explain that I only wanted a relationship with God that did not end with me being hurt and abandoned. I did not have the words to describe this fear to anyone, not this stranger or a trusted friend. I responded by challenging him with the big question I had had about God since I was a child. I had saved the question for this very moment. It was a question I thought no one could answer satisfactorily. "How many people are starving and abandoned in the world, living in mud huts without fresh water and so much disease and suffering? Where is God for them?" I said, believing I would stump this sober, sage older man. It was childish, I admit, but I had formulated the question at a difficult time in my life. It was a concept I clung to to justify why God did not exist in my life and why I never felt safe. Today, I know this big question was really about me: *Where was God for me?*

The old-timer looked at me and smiled. He said that "his" God put unlimited resources on the earth to feed, clothe, and shelter humanity. That there are plenty of resources for all on this earth. God, of his understanding, had placed everything on this planet, yet people have interfered with it and become greedy. Nobody should be starving, but we had made food a commodity to be traded for profit. It's people who block God's gifts that are intended for everyone. The food we waste in this country alone could feed the world. He asked, "How much food do you waste, Tim? How much do you throw away each week?"

The speaker's words profoundly impacted me when he suggested that I could make a difference in the fight against hunger and homelessness. I realized I had a new perspective and a potential role in addressing these issues. He encouraged me to be generous, loving, tolerant, and patient while prioritizing and improving my life. By changing my view and attitude, I could change the world. He believed that by loving our neighbors as we love ourselves, no one would have to suffer from hunger. He urged me to practice humility, forgiveness, and empathy for others, which are essential to his sobriety.

"God is not somewhere out there," he said as he pointed to the sky. "God lives in each of us, right here—" he pointed to his heart. That concept was foreign to me, and I never considered looking at spirituality this way.

Then he said something that hit me hard, "Forgive yourself. Tim, why don't you start there?"

I was dumbfounded because this older gentleman had utterly disarmed me. Somehow, I felt he understood the shame I felt as an alcoholic. I had thought I was putting this guy in his place with my unanswerable question. I was ready to argue the non-existence of God. But I absorbed every word he said and replied, "Just how does all that keep you sober?"

"Keep working on the recovery program with your sponsor and discover this for yourself. When you find a God of your understanding, trust and rely on God to keep you sober. I wish you could see how much God loves you and the potential he sees in you."

He added, "Have you ever considered that God was working behind the scenes and caring for you? Maybe your Higher Power shut you off and got you out of that after-hours club you were in on your last night of drinking."

Before this point, I had never contemplated how God viewed me or how much He loved me. Instead, I clung to assumptions based on my dysfunctional experiences and negative attitude. It was not until I embarked on my journey toward recovery and sobriety that I began to consider that many of my problems stemmed from my perspective, which was filled with fear, anger, and cynicism due to my limited experiences. This new chapter in my life required me to confront the challenging notion that God loved me, which was difficult to accept, considering the fear, shame, and trauma from my childhood that I blamed on him. I had been utterly oblivious to the possibility that a Higher Power had always been there for me. Perhaps all my mother's prayers on my behalf had been answered. With this newfound awareness, I resolved to keep an open mind and continue listening to the stories and advice of people in recovery.

Getting a Recovery Sponsor

When I started attending meetings with the recovery group, I had no idea what a "sponsor" was. One person said, "It is a friend who guides you to recovery." Another offered, "It's someone who has a lot of suggestions for you to follow if you want to stay sober." One older gentleman with many years of sobriety smiled and said, "A sponsor is what people who relapse don't have. So, if you want to pick up a drink again, whatever you do, don't get a sponsor." I wanted to punch him in the face because I received his obvious, simple, logical message and its implications.

After a few months of attending meetings, I found a sponsor: my friend Jack. Jack was from the same neighborhood as me, and we had done a significant amount of drinking and partying together. Remarkably, he had been in recovery for several years. His wisdom and care for people impressed me, so I asked Jack to be my recovery sponsor. He is a living example of how this recovery program works. He was also with me the first time I spoke at a meeting, and I appreciated that.

Jack suggested that I join him in a Recovery Step Study Group. This group would be an opportunity to learn about the twelve steps to get and stay sober. Jack was full of enthusiasm, and he encouraged me to participate. At first, I wanted none of this. I was sure that it wouldn't work for me and that it was not the right time to engage in looking at my life. I came up with many excuses for not attending a Recovery Study Group, even though I had no idea what would occur in the group. Jack observed that my behavior was typical in early recovery; it's called "contempt prior to investigation" and is not uncommon for newly sober people to think this way.

Jack also explained that I was experiencing "self-centered fear," just like he had once before. He had been afraid of the unknown and ready to cut and run—just like me. He suggested I stay and try it and assured me we could do this together.

"Trust your Higher Power to take care of you," he said.

"That's not as easy as it sounds," I muttered. "You just don't understand." How would I explain that I did not want to be hurt or disappointed by God? How could I overcome my childhood trauma and the shame of being an alcoholic? I wrongly let the opportunity to discuss this issue pass without a word of explanation.

Jack explained that the Recovery Study Group had helped him deal with life on life's terms and made him a better person. It was a unique opportunity to learn about yourself and the underlying issues that affected your thoughts, emotions, and actions. More importantly, it enabled him to avoid alcohol and drugs. I could not understand how working the recovery steps would help prevent drinking alcohol. He attempted to explain that alcohol abuse was a *symptom* of everything that was going on in my life. I did not see the connection because, at that time, I struggled with trust, and he was asking me to be vulnerable and trust the recovery process. I thought being vulnerable meant being weak, that you get hurt and disappointed when vulnerable. It is a difficult concept to accept, especially when you are newly sober. However, he was persuasive, so I relented and agreed to try it, with the understanding that I would drop out if it did not work or if I felt uncomfortable.

The group discussions were truthful, extensive, and, at times, intense, which forced me to look inward. This included discovering my motivations and the "underlying causes and conditions" that contributed to my alcohol and drug abuse. That was a daunting assignment, and I held back because of my shame, trauma, and "self-centered fear" that I continued to hold on to.

Early in the process, it was suggested that I look honestly at my resentments and fears, among other emotional issues that have a hold on me. The first task was to write down all my resentments—and I had plenty. I had thirty-six years of bitter resentments to include on my very long and ever-increasing list. I listed my fears and all the people I was angry with. This came quickly because resentment and fears have always been present in my mind, influencing my decision-making. (I once heard someone define Irish Alzheimer's as meaning you never forget a resentment!)

The first time I "worked the steps," I did them to the best of my ability. That meant I held back on a few of my resentments and fears, unable and unwilling to let go. I did not talk about or acknowledge them. Just like when I was a kid, don't talk, trust, or feel emotions.

The instructions for the next step were to share what I could with another person and a God of my understanding. I still had no idea of who or what my God was. I was averse to sharing anything personal or embarrassing with another person. But I wanted to stay sober, so I reluctantly did what was suggested. My desire to remain sober was slowly overcoming my shame, fears, and resentments.

To the best of my ability, I continued with the process. My extensive list exposed a surplus of uncomfortable resentments and painful emotions. I was ready to hand them over to a God of my understanding, so I put the list in my dresser and waited. And waited. I did not do anything except mouth the words and wait. I wasn't challenging my thoughts and emotions or finding gratitude in my life. The resentments and fear randomly appeared in my mind, and I wasn't challenging them.

I persevered and completed the remaining recovery steps, working the program to the best of my ability. However, I still held on to some toxic resentments and struggled with my Higher Power, whom I had not defined. I stayed sober, but I was faking it.

Jack said it was okay to hold onto my resentments, but it was unnecessary and might lead me to relapse and pick up a drink. Even so, I wasn't ready to give up all that resentment because, to some degree, I was conditioned to hold on to them. My relationship with God was minimal at best. Jack told me he had held onto his resentments for many years until a friend offered him some insight.

He said, "Resentments will own and consume you by taking away essential things from you, such as family, friends, relationships, and your Higher Power. You have no idea how much energy you have spent on resentments and the emotional cost to you. Resentments harm your inner peace of mind and impact your ability to love yourself. Wherever you go, your resentments arrive at the same time you do and will creep into any pleasure you seek. Resentment invades, always at the wrong time, and continuously robs people."

I shared with him the many times the past would come into my life and distract me from enjoyment.

He said resentment and self-pity are two sides of the same coin.

I reacted with anger." Are you saying that I'm engaging in self-pity?" I wanted nothing to do with self-pity because that was the easy way out. I was working too hard to sit around and cry; *poor me.*

"No," he said. "I'm saying that I engaged in self-pity over my resentments. I felt terrible because of my resentment. Can you see how this impacted me? Can you see how my resentments and self-pity are two sides of the same coin?"

I could, but I protested that it wasn't me. It took me a long time to finally understand and agree that my resentments and self-pity were two sides of the same coin.

At the end of completing the twelve steps, I felt something was missing. I didn't feel the spiritual awakening mentioned in the twelve steps of this recovery program. *What were they talking about? Maybe God is not listening to me.* I felt everyone else had discovered a pathway to a spiritual connection to God except me. Several group members reported a profound and rapid spiritual awakening. I felt very disappointed because I thought I was doing something wrong or broken beyond repair.

It had taken several months of weekly meetings, but I had completed the recovery program as best I could. Fortunately, my sponsor always reminded me that doing the steps was "to the best of my ability." That concept made my experience much more manageable. And I had done the steps to the best of my ability—which wasn't a hundred percent. I had held back on the things that shamed and embarrassed me. I remained inundated with shame and held on to the anger of my childhood. I didn't fully trust the program, and I certainly didn't trust my Higher Power. I continued attending the meetings and staying sober, but something was missing.

As I continued attending recovery meetings regularly, I became more comfortable in the program. The group members were friendly and always available to offer suggestions and support. I was wise enough to accept this kindness and support. In reality, this was the "last house on the block" that offered a safe harbor for me. I became more involved in the group and took on various responsibilities, such as greeter, coffee maker, bookie, and chairperson. I always helped to put tables and chairs away.

After months of sobriety, I felt incredibly optimistic and confident about myself. I had discovered a way to abstain from drinking, taking it one day at a time. The recovery program was working as it was designed to. To my surprise, I was asked to sponsor a newly sober individual who had recently started attending the group, and I agreed. I shared everything that had been passed along to me about the recovery program, and the newcomer managed to maintain his sobriety. I was surprised, not by his ability to stay sober, but because I never believed that I had anything important to offer another person. The lack of self-esteem I experienced is common among children of alcoholics and active alcoholics.

A "day at a time" turned into twelve months. Remarkably, I had stayed sober for an entire year. Not one drink or drug for 365 days! During the first year of my recovery, I witnessed many people relapse because they stopped attending meetings. I was grateful and astonished at my accomplishment. I was twelve years old the last time I had gone a year without a drink! The night when I received my one-year "chip," two of my sober brothers showed up to support me. It was a special day for me. I had begun to replace fear and resentment with gratitude and felt happy. But I had a lot of work ahead of me. Internal fear and resentment would ebb and flow like the tides on Carson Beach.

After one year of sobriety, I felt good about myself. My resentments and anger had not entirely left me. The grievances I thought my Higher Power would remove from me would return occasionally. I stayed sober, but I had to consider that there was more work to be completed. Was it possible that God was not listening to me because of my unfortunate history? Even so, I was not deterred from attending the weekly recovery meetings. In fact, for some weeks, I would go to multiple meetings daily because it helped me stay sober, and I felt optimistic about my life. I could not deny that my life was improving—not just on the outside but on the inside. The potential to feel even better was there. I started gaining insight into the phrase, "It's an inside job."

I felt good about who I was and confident that my life would continue to get better. My self-esteem was at a high point. The hope, love, truthfulness, and patience I received from my group members encouraged me to avoid alcohol. I continued to be an active participant in the program. I regularly attended meetings; before I realized it, the months of sobriety quickly turned into years of sobriety. Life was good, and I was grateful for the journey I was now on. I began doing fun and exciting things I had only thought about before, such as travel, sailing, hiking, and being there for my family and friends when asked. When drinking, I sat at the bar and only talked about doing things. Life without alcohol is much different and fulfilling in a very good way.

I consciously sought new opportunities and pushed myself out of my comfort zone. I was confident enough to change careers to find more personally satisfying work. I returned to graduate school, completed a second master's degree program, and embarked on a new career in clinical social work. Not bad for a young man held back two years in grammar school and with an erratic and spotty college educational background! I resigned from my full-time job, sold my house, and moved to a new community for a fresh start. Sure, I still had a mortgage and bills to pay, but I gained the confidence to take a risk on things that would improve my life because I was sober. I had steady confidence and a feeling that I would be okay. This was very different from the gloom and doom that had been a large part of my life for a long time and clouded by years of alcohol abuse.

I regularly attended recovery meetings and stayed connected with my sober support network. I knew sobriety had to remain my top priority to continue thriving in my newfound life. It was a delicate balance, but I was determined to make it work. Looking back on my journey, I am amazed at how far I have come. I never could have imagined that I would be where I am today. Sobriety has given me a second chance at life and all it offers. I am forever grateful for the opportunity to live it to the fullest.

The Journey of Recovery Continues

After five years of continuous sobriety, my sponsor, Jack, suggested we join another Recovery Twelve-Step Study Group. "Best not to rest on your laurels," he said. "This is a journey, not a destination, and it's best to have a reality check now and then." So, I joined another group and began the process once again. The truthfulness that was shared in this group was remarkable and very appealing. I was hooked. I completed all the steps, and just like last time, I wrote up my list of resentments and then waited and waited. I waited for my Higher Power to remove these burdensome resentments. But just like the last time, I was guarded and did not venture beyond making a list while waiting for my resentments to be removed. During this time, I maintained sobriety by participating in the group and regularly attending recovery meetings.

I can honestly say that my career and relationships—my life— improved during these years. Physically and emotionally, I was feeling great! More importantly, I was not drinking or using drugs. The shame of being an alcoholic continued dissipating because now I was a "recovering alcoholic." This was due to understanding the disease concept I discovered in the recovery program. I started to grow spiritually and prayed more frequently. My goal was to develop a closer relationship with my Higher Power. It was a struggle, but I continued because the people who came before me had suggested it. I was never all into the "Higher Power thing." Sometimes, I would "fake it 'til I make it,"—which was another suggestion. I knew a spiritual foundation was lacking in my recovery program. Still, I persevered because of the profound hope and trust I found in the program and its people.

I discovered that my emotional struggle was shame and fear-based, often about my past or desire to move on. When it was not about the past, I would obsess about the future, with only an infrequent thought about the here and now. My thoughts were often somewhere else. I grappled with this for many years and repeatedly questioned the benefits of sobriety. I sometimes thought the recovery program was not working for me and that taking that one drink would not make a difference. When I was feeling down, I blamed the people and the program and stayed away from meetings for weeks. I did not forget what I had learned from others who had relapsed—drinking didn't solve any of their problems, and it was as bad as ever when they went out and drank—and I was fortunate to learn through others' mistakes and not so arrogant to think it would be different for me. I was also aware that some people who relapse never return to the recovery program. Fortunately, someone from the group or my sponsor would call me when I was absent from the meeting and ask, "how I was doing." My sponsor would say, "We missed you at last week's meeting. Come on back because you have something to offer the newcomer."

That simple action by another recovering person made me feel valued. I always returned because I genuinely knew in my heart that my way did not work and that something positive in the recovery program did. I needed to find what that "something" was. I also learned that my experiences could be helpful to a new person, and I wanted to give back what had been freely given to me. I relied on the resilience I had developed as a kid, returned to my recovery meetings, and stayed sober. When I had been drinking and using drugs, I went to any lengths to get high. I might as well use that same perseverance to attend recovery meetings. So, I trudged the road, learning to live on life's terms, and I felt optimistic.

However, a spiritual connection remained elusive, even though I was much more open to having a Higher Power. One evening, my sponsor and I discussed my struggle and the lack of a spiritual awakening. A thought hit me as we spoke: *Maybe God was working in my life after all, and I did not see it. Could it be possible that my Higher Power had put the recovery group in front of me and offered hope, love, truthfulness, and patience? Maybe the group was channeling these gifts from my Higher Power.* I concluded that my Higher Power gave me what I needed and not what I wanted, which was the right amount of God's grace to keep me sober and engaged in the recovery program. After all, these values kept me sober so far, which is exactly what my idea of a loving God would provide me. It was intriguing that my recovery group provided just what I needed in the right way and time.

After many years of sobriety, I began to see things differently. The imagination and creativity I had lost as a child returned while my insecurities and irrational fears decreased. I became open-minded and considered other possibilities instead of cutting concepts off at the knees and running away. Positive thoughts and optimism replaced pessimism and negativity. Gratitude and appreciation for the small things in life became more prominent in my thinking. I changed, and it felt good. I was also grateful that I was learning who I was, what my needs were, and how to enjoy myself. I was getting comfortable in my own skin and sensed that I would be okay.

But it was not a constant feeling. My past resentments and anger at Dad and God would come out of nowhere, which was troublesome. It has been many years since Dad passed away. Why couldn't I overcome the scars of trauma, fear, and anger? At times, I hesitated and questioned my motives for staying sober. Yes, I was sober, but occasionally, I would shut down emotionally and feel the terrible, familiar pain and anger of the past. Remarkably, by this time, I had put together decades of sobriety.

At this point in my life, it was evident that my life was very good. I had the humility to know that my life was better than some but not better than all. I had no desire to drink. I acquired many of the material things I wanted, but I had the wisdom to understand that these things would not make me feel better. My relationships with family and friends were going well and becoming stronger every day. Professionally, I have had many good jobs with meaningful and fulfilling responsibilities over the years. I was open to and continued to seek a spiritual relationship with my Higher Power. One thing I did right was not to drink, one day at a time for many days, which turned into additional years of sobriety.

There was a time when I believed I could not live without alcohol. It wasn't until I hit my bottom and admitted that I could not live *with* it. Because of my recovery, my life has exponentially changed for the better. My life has been filled with opportunities that would never have happened if I had kept drinking. The depth and breadth of my life, internally and externally, are remarkable. If I had continued drinking, I am confident I would have ended up incarcerated, living on the streets, or dead like many others from my neighborhood.

Alcohol was a big lie, and it wanted more, unlike sobriety, which gave me a path toward truthfulness, freedom, and much more. Sobriety gave me self-confidence, the freedom to make healthy choices, have real friends and relationships, and the ability to take a healthy risk to improve myself, buy a home, change careers, and be responsible. So, I persevered in recovery and remained sober.

Still Doubting

I cannot deny that I had moments of doubt during my many years of sobriety. Some days, I felt depressed and ungrateful, unable to sense the presence of God. I had misgivings, reexperienced the shame of my past, and resorted to thinking like the traumatized kid I once was. When this happened, one of the group members described me as "off the beam."

While on vacation in Turks and Caicos with a large group of sober people, I again felt disconnected from my Higher Power. I left the resort area and searched for a quiet spot to read a book I had picked up at the airport newsstand, titled *Keep Calm and Trust God*. I thought this book might provide more insight into my struggle. Even though there were three hundred sober people back at the resort willing to help, I decided to walk away and be alone to find a solution—another clear example of my arrogant thinking that I could figure it all out independently. My sponsor, Jack, often said, "Sure, you could get sober alone, but why would you?"

As I walked along the beach, looking for a shady spot, a man emerged from the water and almost bumped into me. He said hi, and I replied likewise. Then he noticed the "Boston Strong" printed across the front of my tee shirt and asked, "Are you from Boston?"

"Yup, sure am. Are you?" I replied.

"I'm from outside of Boston." He was wearing a hat with USMC on it and had tattoos on his arms.

"Are you a Marine?" I asked.

He was, indeed. We talked briefly about some Marines I knew, and I mentioned that both nephews were in the US Marine Corps. He loved hearing that. He then asked if I was staying with all the sober people at the beach resort. When I confirmed, he revealed that he was also in long-term recovery. I told him about the incredible recovery meetings at the resort. I suggested he should drop in on the meeting tonight. All were welcome.

After a few more minutes of small talk, I said, "Well, nice talking to you. I'm going to continue my walk."

Just as I turned away, he asked, "How's your sobriety?"

What? How's my sobriety? Who the heck is he to ask me that? I did not know this guy, and the question seemed too personal. But then I did something totally out of character. I turned back, looked at him, and said, "Not too good."

"Oh? Why not?" he asked.

"It's the God thing," I replied. "I have many years of sobriety, yet I don't feel a meaningful connection with my Higher Power."

I could not believe I had just shared something personal with some random guy I met on the beach. It felt like revealing a national security secret. I might have to silence this guy and bury him in the sand! The familiar feeling of self-centered fear started creeping back. I lowered my head in shame as I waited for his reaction. *Here it comes*, I thought.

"Oh, the God thing. That's the best part of the recovery program," he said with a broad, enthusiastic smile. "It's a gift of recovery. God is a gift, but it's not if you don't accept it. Like at Christmas when someone hands you a present. It's not a gift if you don't take it." He shared with me how grateful he was to have a God of his understanding. "It's a gift of the program," he repeated. "Accept the gift. God keeps us sober. Think about the alcoholics who cannot find a Higher Power and stay sober. God exists for me," he said. "Look at all that is good in the world. Look at this beach. Did man create this? Can a man keep you sober? Did you get yourself sober? How many times did you try to get sober on your own?"

"I lost count," I said.

Then he said, "If you got yourself sober, why didn't you enter the recovery program the day before?"

That comment stung. If I had known what my last night of drinking would be, I would have avoided it at any cost. I nearly took my own life that night.

Then he continued, "Your Higher Power brought you into a recovery program on his terms and no one else's. Accept the gift from God. Remember, it's not a gift if you don't accept it. Accept the gift, Tim."

What the heck? I did not recall telling this guy my name. I must have, but still, it caught me off guard. Surprisingly, I realized I had no shame or fear at that moment. Instead, I felt a profound sense of hope. *He's right,* I thought. I could not refute anything that he said. Once again, the invitation to discover my Higher Power came from a person in recovery. This time, it was a stranger on a beach a thousand miles from home.

If this wasn't a message from my own Higher Power and I did not learn from it, then I thought I must be an idiot and would never find God. The problem was me and my attitude. It was me who was blocking spirituality and a genuine relationship with God. I needed to let go of resentments and fears. I had to accept the gift and run with it. What did I have to lose? It was worth the risk. I had to trust and rely on a God of my understanding. I could handle the disappointment if that's what happens. My confidence and desire for a genuine relationship with God became more robust than my fears of getting hurt. I had to take a leap of faith and see where it would lead me. I could no longer remain blind to God;

instead, I would exercise my choice to accept his presence in my life. After all, recovery is an unmerited gift.

He's right, I thought once again. We shook hands, and I was grateful that I had the opportunity to speak to another recovering alcoholic I met on a beach. As I walked back to the resort, I concluded that my Higher Power, whom I choose to call God today, had placed that man in my life at a critical moment. If that was not God's grace working through another human being, then nothing was. I had never seen or spoken to that man again until years later when I was in Florida speaking at a remote recovery meeting. A man reached out to me and said he "thinks he knows that guy." We talked, and he informed me that he and the guy from the beach attended the same recovery meeting in Massachusetts. What a coincidence. Or was my higher power at work? He gave me his email address, and we reconnected. Thank you, Wayne!

Discovering and Practicing Faith

*No one has ever seen God. Yet, if we love one
another, God remains in us, and his Love is
brought to perfection in us.*
-1 John 4:11-18

I continued participating in the recovery program because it
worked as promised by offering me another day of sobriety. The
people I followed found their sobriety and spirituality, and I was
attracted and wanted more because this was a better way to live.
Freedom from alcohol and the painful carnage it brought upon me
is my reward. I observed how they conducted their lives, living one
day at a time, and the positive results they were experiencing. My
confidence in the recovery program grew stronger each day, year
after year.

I often struggled with my spirituality and asked myself if all
this work was worth the effort. I occasionally questioned the need
to remain abstinent from alcohol. I thought since I had not had a
drink of alcohol for many years, one drink would not hurt me. This
thought of having a drink occurred repeatedly when I did not
participate in the recovery program or felt pessimistic about my
life. When I was in such a state of mind, a friend reminded me that
I was setting myself up for relapse and it would be wise to talk
about this with a sponsor or another recovering alcoholic. He also
shared that his thoughts of drinking would return when he "took
my will back" and moved away from his Higher Power.

I persevered with the program because I feared I would drink
again. After all, my goal was to improve the quality of my inner
spiritual life while maintaining sobriety so that I would never have

to re-experience my last night of drinking and using drugs. The thought of relapse was physically and emotionally terrifying. I know I must never do that again because I cannot survive another one of those lonely, desolate nights.

The people who worked the recovery program and stayed sober possessed a connection to a Higher Power that provided what they needed to live a fulfilling life. Examples were before me, but I did not always see them because of fear, shame, and low self-esteem.

My second sponsor, Paul M., was an example of how someone can live a spiritual life and maintain sobriety. Although Jack was my sponsor for fifteen years, and we remain close friends to this day, Paul M. had a more spiritual way of looking at life, and I was attracted to that. When I told Jack that he was out and Paul was in, we laughed at ourselves because it was like breaking up a romantic relationship. Jack said, "No hard feelings. I'll be here when Paul dumps you." It was a perfect friendship based on the fatal disease that we had. We would do anything to support each other to stay sober one day at a time. Luckily, there are no rules for having a sponsor as long as it is not yourself!

Paul M. taught me many times that a simple gesture of spending a few minutes with another person makes an enormous difference for that person. On one occasion, while leaving an office full of a large group working on a political phone bank. Paul noticed one guy working alone and off to the side making calls. He walked over to the guy to chat with him. Paul knew this young man struggled with learning disabilities and mild autism, appearing odd at times to some people. I watched as Paul spent a few moments of undivided attention on this young man. The guy cheered up and was beaming with pride as Paul put his hand out, thanked him for all his work, and offered to get him a cup of coffee. Every time he saw that young man, Paul stopped what he was doing to spend just a few minutes with him while others ignored him. It was obvious that this made an enormous difference to that person's self-esteem. A gift of a few moments with another person tells them, "I see you, and you matter." For Paul, that was how he practiced his spirituality. This was the God of Paul's understanding working through him.

Paul also had another very spiritual quality. He did not engage in frivolous gossip. "Gossip can be toxic and harmful," he told me. He was wise and had a formula he used before he spoke about someone. He would ask: Is this statement factual, truthful, and helpful to the person? If not, he would ignore the gossip and focus on the person's good qualities. Unlike others, he did not ask what was in it for him when he helped someone. He was selfless, humble, generous, and always doing the next right thing. He understood that we are all imperfect and no better than anyone else. I have noticed this is a common characteristic of spiritual people, who have values like those I imagined my Higher Power would have. Paul was the Good Samaritan who would stop to help the person others ignored. This is what it means to be an instrument of God's peace; anyone may choose this path. Paul passed away recently, but I was grateful to have him as my sponsor. I had to get sober and spiritually well to encounter and appreciate people like Paul. I can confidently say that my favorite bartender and drug dealer never possessed the virtues that Paul and others in recovery have.

I was a recipient of this same kindness very early in my recovery. The sincerity of another sober person's simple, sincere question—"Tim, how are you doing today?"—would move me.

When someone went out of their way to ask if I wanted a cup of coffee, I would feel their kindness. "Good to see you again, Tim," would make me feel welcomed and valued. Simple gestures such as these are life-changing and transformative to a fragile person in the early stages of recovery. I had to allow people to let me feel loved and appreciated rather than push them away because of my insecurities. All simple acts of kindness by other recovering alcoholics attracted me and encouraged me to continue with the program. Their passion and care were genuine. I could feel the presence of something bigger than me, and I wanted more. I did not know it then, but this was my Higher Power, working through other people, helping me stay sober and grow into the person I was supposed to be.

I feel connected and grateful when someone does a simple act of kindness for me. It isn't easy to describe, yet I know it explicitly when I experience it. This kindness attracted me and encouraged me to stay with the recovery program. It was those simple acts of kindness and love that were the very beginning of my loving myself. People would tell me, "Let us love you until you can love yourself."

The beauty of the presence of God is that I believe we all have the ability to place ourselves in that sweet spot by thinking of others and eliminating our egos, fears, attachments, self-centeredness, and resentments. Today, we have a choice to live in the light of recovery and hope rather than being that person who lives alone, in the dark shadows of alcohol and drug abuse. Remarkably, when I live in that sweet spot, I stay sober. I have felt it and witnessed this phenomenon in recovery repeatedly.

It took many years of sobriety before I fully believed and accepted that my Higher Power actually cared for me. One afternoon, the truth came to me powerfully while I was napping in a hammock in my garden. Oddly enough, I was dreaming about the gospel story in Mark 5, a story of a woman who was convinced that if she could only touch the hem of the cloak of Jesus, she would be healed. I had heard this reading in a priest's homily months before. It was strange that I would think about the gospel while napping because that is so unlike me. I pictured myself in this scene as I watched the woman push through the crowd to touch the garment of Jesus. I imagined she was aggressive, shoving people out of the way to feel the garment, like a fearless girl from the projects in Southie. I admired that! She reached to touch the hem of his cloak, and Jesus told her, "Your faith has healed you."

I thought to myself, *what faith she has! I wish that my mediocre faith was as strong as hers.* Then, I suddenly realized I believed in what this woman had done. She knew that she would be healed when she touched the garment of Jesus. I thought that if I could touch Jesus's garment, I would recover from my alcoholism. God would do for me what I could not do for myself. I sat up in the hammock with a wide smile. I felt indescribably peaceful. I knew I had faith when I believed I could touch the cloak and be saved. *That is faith*, I said to myself. *You do have faith! I am not broken and damaged goods!* The interior shame I carried with me of who and what I thought I was disappeared. I had finally found my elusive spiritual awakening. I cherish this moment because today, faith is an essential part of my recovery journey.

That was the moment when I embraced the gift of having God in my life. Just as the Marine I encountered on the beach suggested, that is faith, and at that very moment, I experienced it. I have found the faith I had been seeking and felt immense comfort and gratitude. This faith had resided within me all this time. I needed to stop viewing the world through the lens of pain, shame, resentment, and fear. I had to shift my attitude, practice forgiveness, and open my heart. That is the inner work that people referred to when I embarked on my recovery journey many years ago.

I know I will never physically touch the actual cloak of Jesus, yet I believe such an act would heal me. This shift in my perspective was deeply profound. I was overwhelmed with a sensation of happiness and confidence, and I knew I would be alright. I felt as though my membership had been accepted into an extraordinarily exclusive club. From that day forward, I believed everything in my life would ultimately fall into place.

I now understood what the woman in my recovery group meant when she asked me more than twenty-five years ago, "Can you believe that I believe?" She showed me her faith in her Higher Power and the recovery program. I could only be a skeptical bystander, not a believer at that time. I was a bystander in the crowd, watching others recover from alcoholism. I had too much pain, fear, and a lack of trust to believe, and the best I could do was say that I believed that she believed.

Believing in her spirituality was the start of a pivotal change in my recovery journey. It was a humbling recognition that I did not understand anything about spirituality or God until I saw it with my own eyes in the people who participated in the recovery groups. Then, once I witnessed and understood that it was available for me, I never wanted to let it go. I found a peaceful and spiritual way to live. Today, I am full of gratitude. A spiritual life thrives inside me and is evident in my thoughts and actions.

Today, I believe in a God of my understanding, resulting in a profound change of focus and direction in my prayers. I no longer pray for things to happen or to obtain something for my benefit. I pray to change my attitude and outlook on the world around me, to be of service and not self-seeking or full of fear. This is also the "inside work" suggested when I first entered the recovery program. I have stopped blocking myself from God so I may do his will, not mine. I stopped looking for God "out there," and instead, I examined my inner self. It is time to move forward and find my desired sobriety and path to freedom. It is time to take a risk and turn my will and care over to a God of my understanding. It is time for me to do the next right thing! Before this time, I was experiencing life on the exterior and not the inner, where I met a God of my understanding.

Blame Games No More

Accepting my Higher Power was not the only inside job I had to accomplish. After twenty-eight years of sobriety, I listened to a man named Beau share the experience of his recovery journey at a meeting. He talked about his experiences as a teenager with his alcoholic mother and how, after many years, he was finally free of her emotional shadow. "Free from the deep scars left by my abuser," he said. I perked up, anxious to finally hear the key to the emotional contentment I lacked.

I was still looking for the answer to my problems and the key to contentment, so when I heard this speaker, I was excited and prepared to listen to his method and sage advice. But when he said the key was forgiveness, I could not help but feel cheated. *Bullshit,* I thought. *I have heard this a thousand times at recovery meetings across the United States and in the hundreds of self-help and spirituality books I have read.* I initially rejected it as an overused cliché.

However, this guy was different in his persona, disposition, demeanor, and calmness. He was authentic, sincere, and convincingly free from his tormentor. He had some spirituality about him. He was the real deal. I considered contacting him to discuss how he had accomplished this forgiveness. A week later, I contacted the group secretary to get the list of group members. Still, after I received his contact information, I did what I usually do: procrastinate. I "chickened out." What was I going to ask him? My self-centered fear kicked in. I felt like a coward with inept communication skills, embarrassed, and paralyzed. Weeks went by as I went about my business—putting together my thoughts, preparing for my day-to-day work, signing on to seemingly never-ending remote online recovery meetings until I received a private message one day. It was from the guy who had talked about forgiveness! He attempted to contact a group member with the same first name as mine.

"You've got the wrong Tim," I texted in the chat.

He apologized, promising to find the "correct" Tim, and, just like that, we both turned our attention back to the online meeting. As the meeting wrapped up, I could not get over the shock of discovering that the person I wanted to speak with had reached out to me accidentally. *Is this just a coincidence, or is God working through this guy?*

I thought about texting him. Yet again, I was awash in self-centered fear of asking stupid questions, feeling inferior, and being embarrassed. I wrestled with unanswerable questions. *Was this some sort of sign? Was his text just that, a coincidence?* I had to know.

I asked to speak with him at the next recovery meeting we attended. I explained my interest in his talk from the previous month. Without hesitation, he gave me his phone number. Our conversation lasted over an hour, and he talked about the fourth and fifth steps of the twelve-step program. He insisted that to do it right, you must write down all your resentments, look at each one, and be willing to try forgiveness. Complete all the twelve steps, but pay particular attention to steps eight and nine as you grow. Step nine is about making amends.

At first, I balked. My self-righteous pride kicked in. *How dare he*, I thought. But I had to admit that I had never thoroughly completed the fourth step in my many years of sobriety. Intellectually, I had done a walk-through of all the steps, including the fourth and fifth steps, with my sponsor. In fact, I stood before a large group of other recovering alcoholics and proclaimed that I had completed all the steps. In reality, I never entirely accepted my past or forgiven my tormentor. I did not feel acceptance or forgiveness for my Dad or God. I felt shame, resentment, anger, abuse, and that I had been short-changed. Once again, I looked good on the outside while I was raging on the inside. I lost count of how often I was reminded that getting well is "an inside job."

From this conversation, I finally realized I had to learn to forgive to move on with my life. It was clear that I had to take the necessary steps to finally let go of the past, free myself to live life, and become the person I was supposed to be. It was time for me to be the authentic person God created. It was a complicated process, but I started by forgiving myself for my past mistakes and impulsive, poor decisions. Then, I gradually worked towards forgiving others, including those who had caused me significant pain and trauma. It was a slow process, and I had to work on it continuously. Still, I eventually found a sense of peace and contentment I had never experienced before.

This guy told me that once he forgave his mom and accepted his childhood experiences, he discovered he could leave his past behind and move on. He was free and no longer carried the resentments, shame, and anger of growing up in an alcoholic's home. He convinced me that he was now free to live and be the person God created him to be because of forgiveness.

He said that if I wanted to reach the point of belief, it was essential to act "*as if.*" He said I must act "*as if*" my Higher Power had done what you asked him to do. "If you have a resentment that you handed over to your Higher Power, why take it back? If you have a negative thought, challenge it and change your viewpoint."

I wanted to be liberated from the anger I had been burdened with for so long. So, I listened and learned. I earnestly wanted to follow his guidance and do what he did. I began by taking small, manageable steps, such as challenging my thoughts. My first thought is usually more of a reaction, which is not always positive or helpful. I tend to think negatively that something will not work, and this goes on unless I have had experience with a situation and am sure of the outcome. I asked myself: *Could I instead decide what my second thought would be? Could I challenge my first thought and ask myself if something had happened before? Were there other possible outcomes if I made another choice?*

I decided to keep an open mind to other possibilities based on the here and now, not on some painful past or possible future. Under the care and guidance of my Higher Power, I changed my thoughts and considered other positive and hopeful possibilities. I discovered that my Higher Power lives in the here and now.

From my discussions with others in recovery, I learned to recognize when my thinking is unproductive. Often, my thoughts were misguided instincts based on self-centered fear, pride, and resentment. Engaging in this behavior leads to anger, shame, bitterness, self-pity, and insecurity. In the past, this type of thinking led to a drink. And it usually occurred when I was judging another person, intolerant, impatient, or not doing the next right thing.

I learned that if I take a moment to think things through, I can change my thoughts and behavior and feel much better about myself and others. More importantly, this is doing the "inside work" to get and stay sober. This shift in my thought process connected me to my Higher Power that, for years, had eluded me. I'm thinking and acting more spiritually now. I imagine how much God loves me and sees me precisely how I want to be loved. It's a great feeling. That is doing the work I refused to do for many years. I admit it is not always easy because sometimes I get stuck in the past. Then again, it is like falling off a horse. You have to get back on!

The gentleman I contacted suggested I work the recovery steps again, paying particular attention to my thoughts this time. "Be honest about your feelings," he said, reminding me I was already aware of my character defects, self-pity, and resentments. "No need to prepare another list of those," he said.

I had been holding on to my list of resentments for years, and it was time to free myself. It was time to decide to "ask God to remove my shortcomings consciously"— and start acting as if they were removed.

"How do I act as if they are removed?" I asked.

"Enjoy that feeling that comes with it. After all, peace and healing come in moments. So, enjoy the moment. Change your thoughts if you start feeling angry because of something long ago. "Move a muscle-change a thought," he said. The past is not in the here and now. Bring yourself to the present. You are in control of your thoughts and associated reactions. Remember that you have handed your anger over to your Higher Power. Why hold on to it? Why get angry if it has been removed? This is where faith comes into your life. These things are removed because you asked your Higher Power to remove them. Just do not go there. You have that ability. Move on and replace that thought with something you choose, such as practicing gratitude or service to another recovering alcoholic. It is a much better feeling."

I could act as if my painful thoughts had been removed. After all, they are only thoughts. I can recognize them before turning them into unpleasant emotions or regrettable actions. This method is much different than before when I placed my character defects list in my desk drawer and waited for my Higher Power to do the work. I needed to take responsibility for my role to do my part.

I have learned that I am responsible for my thoughts and reactions and how to control them. I can control how I respond and react with integrity. It is not always easy, but I catch myself and return to the here and now. My mind should not dwell on the past or the future. When I am angry or depressed, I need to change and find something to be grateful for. This is the work that I must do if I want to stay sober. I sincerely worked on these issues, keeping an open mind and knowing I must change. My attitude and thinking must be available to other possibilities and toward a God of my understanding. God of the here and now must be a part of this.

Researchers can show that many factors contribute to a person developing an addiction. These contributing factors include a person's socioeconomic environment, traumatic experiences, psychic wounds, parent's substance abuse, poor school achievement, and family dysfunction, to name a few. Others believe nature or genetic flaws in the brain, gender, or mental disorders lead to addiction. Often, alcoholism seems to run in families as it does in mine.

The bottom line is that we do not understand whether alcoholism is caused by nurture or nature. But my job is not to dwell on how my addiction developed but to focus on the solution. Engaging in self-pity feeds the opposing forces of addiction. For this recovering alcoholic, it is essential to move past the trauma and dysfunction and to focus on the solution. That's where the gift of recovery can be found. I continuously work towards the solution and do not dwell on or live in the past.

I no longer blame Dad for my life's experiences because he was a sick man trapped by his demons and this disease. I do not blame his fellow firefighters who drank with him or looked the other way when he engaged in unacceptable behavior. I do not blame the supervisors responsible for upholding rules and regulations for the department when they could have interrupted Dad's drinking. I do not blame my teachers or academic counselors either because they didn't know the extent of my traumatic experiences at home. I do not blame the Monsignor who mercilessly shamed an academically struggling fifth-grade outcast who "wasn't from the parish." (Although I wish I did light his car on fire. That would have been something. Haha, just kidding!)

The one person who harmed me more than anyone else was myself. I drank excessively and used drugs when I had other choices. I did not bother to learn and try healthy ways to handle life when I had the opportunity. I did not ask for help when it was available. I took myself to dark, sordid places, looking for companionship and pleasure. I placed myself in dangerous situations under the influence of alcohol and drugs when I knew it was wrong and contrary to my values. I was completely aware that drinking excessively, acting out, taking unnecessary risks, jeopardizing my career, and driving under the influence were wrong. The list is long. But I continued with this behavior, and my alcohol abuse took me to a place where I hated myself and thought that ending my life was the solution.

When I found the solution of not drinking a day at a time, I was obligated to break the cycle of alcoholism and become a better person—a true friend to myself. If I want to be there for another person, I must be there for myself. It all starts and ends with me. I can be the responsible and loving adult in my life. I can offer my experience and knowledge to teach others to stay sober. What a gift! Nobody can accept and share this gift but me. I am blessed to have so many others who lived an alcohol-fueled life and then changed to become better people, their true selves. These people helped change my life, and I am eternally grateful for them.

PART III

Doing the Inside Work

Your image of God creates you—or defeats you.
There is an absolute connection between how we
see God and how we see ourselves and the
universe.
Richard Rohr

As you read this book, I hope you will discover the
transformative miracle that altered my life. While some individuals
may have found this solution in a much shorter timeframe, it took
me many years to uncover it. It took 28 years of maintaining
sobriety and achieving emotional freedom before I could
understand and fully embrace the message of hope and find a
solution to my troubles. Please do not be disheartened by my
timeline because I gained significant growth and happiness during
my journey. I remained committed to sobriety and underwent a
profound change as the process unfolded. The reward of my
perseverance was invaluable and well worth the wait. Just as I was
told it would be when I first entered the recovery program, I have
experienced the truth that my life improves with each passing day
that I choose not to drink.

Like the Wizard of Oz told the Tin Man, he had the heart he
had been searching for all along. I discovered that happiness was
also within me, waiting for acceptance and forgiveness to unlock
it. The interior connection to spirituality was always there, but what

prevented me from experiencing it were the dark clouds of self-loathing, shame, fear, and anger that increased with every drink, leading me to utter those dreaded words, "I did it again."

As someone who spent too many times listing my justification for disliking myself, the soft-spoken members of my recovery group repeatedly invited me in with a simple message, "Let us love you until you can love yourself." At first, I was shocked that they understood my deepest secret. How could they know I had never learned to love myself? How did they understand the emotional pain I experienced? Vainly, I believed that I was somehow unique in my suffering.

These recovering alcoholics had been in that same pit of despair, self-loathing, and loneliness as me. I had tried connecting with people, but my shadow haunted me. At first, I could not relate. But my newly found notion of a compassionate God shifted within.

What I thought was the last step of the recovery process turned out to be my first step to a new way of life. Completing the 12 Steps was the start of a new journey for me. It is not about surviving one more day without alcohol; instead, it is about living a single day with gratitude, as if that is all you have. This means connecting with a Higher Power to experience the gift I have received and to witness the light of hope every day.

I could never have been able to complete this journey on my own. I acquired inner spirituality by working with my group through the 12 steps of the recovery program. I established a relationship with a Higher Power who loves me unconditionally and desires me to experience that love. I finally dropped the pain and resentment I had been carrying. First, I needed to accept the "gift." Something had to go to open the door to peace and love. I had to do the "inside work" and be committed to it.

The "Inside work" means letting go of what prevents you from enjoying your gift of life. It is a humbling experience, not a humiliating one. I committed to doing the inside work at the suggestion of others who are successful in their sobriety. I easily recognize those who have been through it because of their humility, spirituality, and willingness to help. I get the feeling that they feel loved by their higher power. Distorted instincts, anger, or fear do not control these individuals as they once tormented me. They are happy, content, humble, grateful, and free. They have mastered their interior lives and are eager to share their knowledge. They choose to live a day at a time and never have to speak those dreaded words, "I did it again." I wanted this from my sobriety and knew I had to do the work.

Fortunately, I was never alone throughout this journey. Countless individuals have completed the steps and were eager to share their hard-earned knowledge. The recovery people I have encountered on this journey played a crucial role in my success. Through the fellowship, I cleaned up my side of the street. This enables me to share my harrowing journey with the hope that someone, even a single person, can see a better version of themselves and learn to accept their gift.

Allow me to share some of that knowledge with you. As a recovering alcoholic, the following items are critical to my internal journey. I consider this to be my road map to recovery.

Gratitude

The phrase "A grateful heart will never drink" is often repeated at recovery meetings. I was initially skeptical about its significance to my sobriety. These were only words without much wisdom or depth for me. "Yeah, sure, I'm grateful," I'd say. Big deal! Let's move on. I focused on finding the quick fix for my addiction and emotional pain. Little did I realize that my impatience—also known as "I want what I want when I want it," denied me an essential part of sobriety: savoring the gift of gratitude. I did not fully appreciate the role that gratitude could play in my recovery.

What did gratitude have to do with my emotions? What was the connection between gratitude and fear, doubt, and insecurity? My sponsor said, "A grateful heart will never drink. Isn't that why we are here? If you find gratitude, your attitude will start to change. You can slow down and enjoy the rewards of sobriety, friends, family, career, life, and God. These amazing gifts help keep us sober." He explained that a grateful frame of mind could change our attitudes and perspectives, allowing us to experience more joy and contentment. This idea interested me because the concerns that shadowed me from childhood into adulthood are the same negative emotions that occasionally walk with me today. I would love to leave them back in my youth where they belong.

The more I practice gratitude, the more it becomes a natural habit. I appreciated the people and things I often took for granted. I now recognize gratitude's role in helping me overcome my addiction. I practice this habit of gratitude just like I practiced my habit of drinking. Daily! The more I drank, the more I wanted. Today, I try to savor and appreciate everything that makes me grateful. When I choose to do the inside work, my life will become more manageable and enjoyable. The conflict and emotional pain in my mind subside, and gratitude frees me from anger and resentment and opens the door to other possibilities.

One of my favorite quotes is from Cicero (106 BC-43 BC), who said: "Gratitude is not only the greatest of virtues but the parent of all others." Embracing gratitude transformed my life and has made me rediscover and appreciate things I had previously taken for granted. When drinking, I selfishly neglected many virtues that were once important to me. However, I rediscovered these virtues and now strive to practice them daily. Living an honest life enables me to maintain my dignity and face myself in the mirror with humility.

Today, I am grateful and try to acknowledge everything in my life that I would not have had if I had continued drinking and using drugs. Resentments deserve no place in my heart, so I choose gratitude. I focus on life's blessings and try to be of service to others who are struggling.

Gratitude has enhanced my outlook, and I now look at people on the same journey with compassion and patience because I know how they feel. I allow them to tell their story and try to be of service to them, which frequently means listening to what others have experienced, including the trauma and misfortunes they have experienced.

In recovery, many say, "It's easier to act yourself into a new way of thinking than to think yourself into a new way of acting." My thinking is not perfect, but I have always been a good actor, so I do the work each day practicing the gift of gratitude. This approach has made a remarkable difference in my life, and I am grateful for every day that I can stay sober and enjoy the gift of gratitude.

Empathy

Forgiving my Dad was a daunting task that I attempted many times without success. I wondered if my pain was too deep or the emotional wounds too severe. Perhaps I was too angry to forgive and still wanted to punish him. Trapped in a stalemate, I believed I would only be disappointed if I let my guard down and expressed empathy. I am sure all these things were blocking me, but I had to try a different way to forgive if I wanted to be free. Appreciating my Dad's past and the experiences that shaped him as a person allowed me to empathize with him and helped me to understand his behavior better.

My Dad was raised by a single mom who lost her husband, brother, and father during the same week of the Spanish Flu pandemic of 1918. His mother's entire support system and his family of origin suddenly disappeared. My grandfather was a postmaster in Boston with a steady middle-class income that vanished in a day; there were no survivor benefits or other sources of income. My father was two months old when this happened, and my grandmother had two young children to raise alone at a time when society treated women as second-class citizens and provided limited resources. Poverty and hopelessness were widespread during this time, and these challenging circumstances shaped my father's childhood.

When the Great Depression hit, my Dad was eleven years old. He was fifteen when it ended. How did these setbacks impact him during his critical developmental years? What fears, doubts, and insecurities did his single mom introduce to him? Were these character traits passed down to my brothers and me? He grew up in a time of great uncertainty, where many people worried about where they would get their next meal or where they would live. Who was my Dad's role model then? There were limited work opportunities, and many were unemployed and struggled to survive. This was the context that my father and his brother experienced as youngsters.

Despite his flaws, my role model worked two jobs to give us what he believed was his primary duty as a parent. Dad provided a roof over our heads, food, clothing, and family values. To his credit, he did that to the best of his ability.

My father was also impacted by World War II when he was nineteen years old. I recall him telling my brothers and me that he was working at a steel mill in the Hyde Park neighborhood of Boston when he heard over the radio that the US had declared war. He knew he had to enlist and prepare for war. What was that like for a nineteen-year-old? He did not have a father to talk to and seek advice. How is all of this emotionally processed and addressed? If that were me, I would have done what I enjoyed the most: drinking with my friends and getting hammered for days.

He enlisted in the Navy and served in the Southwest Pacific theater but seldom talked about his wartime experience. He had tattoos on his arms that he acquired in the Navy. The tattoo was a Navy anchor with Mom's and his name underneath. They were high school sweethearts separated by the war. The tattoo was a testament to their love for each other.

After the war, my Dad became a firefighter. He endured frequent traumas, including the devastating loss of his brother firefighters at the Vendome Hotel fire. Dad might have appeared calm outside to the neighbors, but he had his demons, as we all do. He turned to alcohol to cope with his pain, just like I did. I now recognize that he did his best to hold onto his values as a person with the disease of alcoholism was capable of doing. I also must accept that "you can't get a hug from a man with no arms."

As I reflect on my father's life, I gain a deeper appreciation of the challenges he faced and the choices that he made. I realized that he did the best he could with the tools he had, and his struggles with alcohol were the result of this disease. Finding empathy for my father allowed me to forgive him and find peace and serenity in my life. Through my recovery program, I learned that empathy is a powerful tool to help us find forgiveness and healing. Empathy is among the many rewards of the recovery program.

Forgiveness

Forgiveness can be a challenging and painful process, particularly for those who have been traumatized. I often wondered why I should pardon someone when, in my mind, I was an innocent victim in this story. Am I responsible for anyone else's drinking? I was a kid trying to figure out his place in a dysfunctional world. The truth is on my side. I did not create my childhood environment. I certainly did not cause anyone to take a drink.

Then again, my experiences of growing up in an alcoholic home are mine. Those were the cards I was dealt. This is who I am and part of the narrative I own today. My responsibility is to examine these experiences, breaking them down into perspectives, taking the good and discarding the bad. While the past is a nice place to visit, it is not a good place to live.

What happened long ago cannot be undone. The negative thoughts and emotions provide no value for me. They cloud my thinking, constrict my feelings, and bring me back to painful memories I do not wish to re-experience. Today, I understand how this dysfunction played a role in my alcoholism and unhealthy character traits that will lead me back to a drink unless I take positive actions to alter myself.

The trap of perpetual victimhood should not define me or hold me back. The opportunity to transform and create the life I want is within reach as long as I stay away from alcohol. I sincerely believe this today, and I recognize that developing a spiritual relationship changed me, making me a better person. A healthy emotional, physical, and spiritual way of living is what I have been seeking throughout my journey. My goal is to have a loving Higher Power in my life and to love and be loved.

How does a person move on from the painful events that shaped them? The idea of forgiveness kept drawing me back to my youth's chaos and emotional pain. As I think about God in this process, I keep asking, Where is He? How do I find room for healthy spirituality in my heart? Thoughts of the here and now were frequently pushed aside and replaced with the insanity of long-ago events. As I recalled past incidents, my anger increased, bringing those negative emotions back into the present. Sometimes, these thoughts from the past gave me heart palpitations, tightened my back muscles, caused migraines, and ruined my day. Reliving the past can sometimes be overwhelming, and my brain wants to "cut and run" and take a drink. Dad is long gone from this world, but the ripples of his actions still run through my life if I let them.

Early in recovery, emotions rose as though my tormentor was present when I attempted to initiate forgiveness. Replaying those tapes, I hoped for different outcomes, but nothing changed.

My father's experiences were his story, not mine. I needed to untangle myself from his disease and get on with my life. Character traits had to be sorted out, the healthy ones identified and put to good use, and the unhealthy ones, such as not talking, trusting, or feeling, discarded. The opportunity to better myself and create the life I want is within reach if I stay away from alcohol and change my thinking. I continually remind myself that If I don't change, alcohol will destroy me!

A healthy emotional, physical, and spiritual way of living is what I strived to achieve on this journey. Letting go of the past and forgiving is not easy. Rumination of the past makes me anxious and depressed at times. Today, I understand that forgiveness alleviates personal suffering and improves mental well-being. The rewards are worth the effort.

Initiating forgiveness is a personal choice and should not be based on whether the person who caused harm is remorseful or admits to any wrongdoing. I hold the power to forgive my Dad. He does not get to have a say in his forgiveness or whether the incidents happened or not. I set the terms and conditions of forgiveness because this impacts me, not him. I can stop this emotional pain if I dare to let go of the past and hand my resentments to a God of my understanding. Letting go of the past and opening the door to my Higher Power is how to initiate forgiveness.

Forgiveness liberates the victim. Forgiveness leads to better self-awareness, helps me find my humanity, and, in some remarkable way, releases me from the pain and resentment caused by my tormentor. This is the doorway into a spiritual relationship I, unfortunately, blocked for many years.

Anger, resentment, and sadness will creep back into my life occasionally. I am only human. Fortunately, as time passes, it is not as intense when it does return, and I know exactly what to do. I look at the big picture, seeking progress, not perfection. I will speak with another person in recovery, where we can reason things out, ultimately freeing me from my painful experiences and achieving the freedom that only forgiveness can bring.

Today, I make healthy choices as a recovering adult and decide what kind of day I will have. I always strive for a grateful heart. When I resit the act of forgiveness, like I battled my alcoholism, my anger and resentments become more intense. As I continue my recovery journey, I strive to forgive, knowing this is the way to achieve freedom.

When I think back at my Dad's life and my own, I see two men suffering from the disease of alcoholism, two who lost the ability to say no to a drink, and two men who had to say, "I did it again." Alcoholism controlled my Dad, taking over his emotions and crushing his values and spirit. We are similar in this regard. After all, I am my father's son.

After learning about the insidiousness of alcoholism, I now have an understanding and empathy for other alcoholics, including myself. If I am going to forgive my alcoholic self, I must find compassion and forgiveness for another alcoholic. Several members of the recovery program suggested: "that you never harm another alcoholic, and when the opportunity arises, you help them if you are able." I was aware of my behavior when I drank, and I felt shame, guilt, and remorse. But it did not stop me. I am confident it was the same for Big John. I know this because I often witnessed his profound shame and guilt.

My friends in the recovery program taught me that forgiveness is one of the most valuable gifts I can give myself. To do this, I had to identify my shortcomings, character defects, and resentments and accept my powerlessness over alcohol to be free. Only then could I work on the other areas of my life, including the understanding that I can pardon others. It takes courage to forgive someone. Anger and self-righteousness are weak excuses not to forgive another person. I also cannot let the threat of imagined humiliation and disappointment block me from forgiveness.

This process took a long time, but that's okay. I am here and grateful for that. I'm free from living with the pain of events and circumstances of long ago. Today, I am free from the trauma, misguided instincts, and dysfunctional thinking I engaged in for so long. The dysfunction that ruled my life has been eliminated and replaced with a healthy understanding that there are steps I can take to be joyous and free to be my authentic self. I can stroll on the beach without reliving the trauma from years past. Forgiveness has given me freedom from the disease of alcoholism and all its menacing dysfunction. Forgiveness now enables me to let go of the past, live in the present, and move confidently into the future, one day at a time. Forgiveness is freedom and opens the door to achieving what I ultimately desire: a spiritual relationship with God of my understanding.

To the best of my ability, I am living one day at a time by tapping into the wisdom of the Prayer of St. Francis and asking my Higher Power to make me an instrument of his peace. Bringing faith, hope, truth, and joy into my world allows me to shine as a beacon of light. Through practicing forgiveness, we receive forgiveness, which is a small price to pay for release from the bitter resentments of the past. Peace of mind cannot be purchased, and living in the light is entirely up to me. This simple prayer of St. Francis is my guide to finding peace of mind:

Prayer of St. Francis

> Lord, make me an instrument of your peace:
> where there is hatred, let me sow love;
> where there is injury, pardon;
> where there doubt, faith;
> where there is despair, hope;
> where there is darkness, light;
> and where there is sadness, joy.
> O Divine Master, grant that I may not so much seek
> to be consoled, as to console,

to be understood, as to understand,
to be loved, as to love.
For it is in giving that we receive,
it is in pardoning that we are pardoned,
and it is in dying that we are born to eternal life.

Acceptance

The experiences that have shaped me, my successes and failures, have provided me with numerous opportunities for personal growth and development. My life has been rich with excitement, challenges, and rewards. I am confident that I can confront any obstacles that come my way, respond appropriately, or choose not to respond at all. When I stumble, I see it as a chance to learn and grow rather than a source of shame.

Doing things my way is no longer as important as it once was. I no longer feel the need to jump into conflicts and control everything. Problems arise when I react to situations based on my selfish desires. Allowing another person's Higher Power to intervene and handle the situation is the most liberating aspect of my recovery. I can not get enough of it because the process has become a source of immense satisfaction and peace.

At the meetings, I would see slogans, such as "Live and Let Live," "One Day at A Time," and "Let Go and Let God," displayed on the walls behind the speaker podium. I arrogantly viewed these phrases as clichés and unimportant until I eventually grasped their simple but powerful wisdom. This realization has had a life-changing effect on me. I developed a more realistic perception of what was happening in the world around me and let go of my need for control. As a result, my stress, anger, and resentment diminished, and I became more patient and compassionate. That is who I believe I am meant to be, and it is yet another gift of my recovery. Knowing that I cannot control things, but my Higher Power can is what I consider true acceptance.

I had to take a massive leap of faith to embrace the recovery program fully. Living a virtuous life is what I desire and deserve. Living as an active alcoholic and drug abuser, consumed by fear and uncertainty, was not my purpose for being on this earth and not the reason for my existence. To achieve my goal, I had to start living like a sober person, thinking like a sober person, and believing in a Higher Power like a sober person. I have found that doing my best to act with integrity, dignity, and honor was how to improve my self-esteem. These qualities are all within me, and I strive to incorporate them into my everyday life. I must act as if these values are genuine and happening in the here and now of my life. I may not be responsible for the first thought which enters my mind. I am responsible for the second and how I choose to respond. Challenging my beliefs and replacing my negative or counterproductive thoughts with healthy and hopeful ones is within my power.

Empathy, forgiveness, gratitude, and acceptance are fundamental to maintaining my sobriety, requiring conscious effort and decision-making. By following these principles, I have opened the door to spirituality and a relationship with my Higher Power, which helps me to stay sober.

Fear and the Three Frogs

"Prayer is taking your fears to God's altar. Faith
is leaving them there."
—Anonymous

Fear is an innate instinct that we all possess, with each having our individual experiences in its development and our reality of how we respond to each situation. Anthropologists assert that fright allows us to make rapid decisions needed for survival, commonly referred to as a "fight or flight" response. This instinct can be rational or irrational, depending on our experiences and responses. Overwhelming fear hinders imagination, extinguishes hope, and stifles creativity. My brain grew like everyone else's during my childhood. Yet, my developmental experiences with fear were often paralyzing and certainly not the norm.

In retrospect, I now understand that my fear was natural, given the unpredictable nature of my father's behavior. I never knew who would come walking through the front door of our home each night: the good man or the drunk dad capable of bursting into a rage with the distorted face, reeking of whiskey, and the fierce-looking eyes of a wolf on the hunt. At other times, he was exhausted from working two jobs while trying his best to smile as he entered his home, seeking rest before getting up and repeating his demanding day. Nevertheless, I needed to be vigilant to react, survive, and maintain the peace to protect my Mom and younger brothers.

As a result of the intensity, duration, and frequency of the fear and anxiety I experienced, I became hypervigilant and overly sensitive to people and the things around me. I learned to "fly under the radar" to avoid conflict. Survival requires independence and adaptability because there is fear and risk of disappointment and abandonment when relying too much on others. At the same time, being a re-actor and not an actor or active participant in my life is necessary due to my lack of confidence and self-esteem.

These survival skills followed me into adulthood, with constant worry ruling my life and guiding my decisions. I avoided risk and never considered the future because I believed it was either full of greatness or utter failure and humiliation. Fear also taught me that things would never improve. I became trapped in my emotional world, unable to envision other possibilities. I became emotionally dysfunctional because I could not trust any other option.

I turned to alcohol to temporarily remove the conflicting and emotional pain I experienced. Alcohol permitted me not to care about anything troubling or upsetting. Alcohol temporarily removed the emotional distress I carried with me. I encountered a better world when I was drinking and getting high. Alcohol became the therapist and friend I trusted and relied upon for comfort and relief. Drinking felt right and eliminated my fears and became my solution and medication. It was a safe harbor in stormy seas.

Sadly, this short-term solution to an ever-growing problem is why my favorite drink was "the next one." I never overcame my debilitating fears by drinking. Still, it calmed my anxieties, blocked the pain, and falsely inflated my self-esteem.

Even after I stopped drinking, I still lived in fear. People in my recovery group suggested that to eliminate fear from our lives, we needed a Higher Power to take all our worries away. "If we ascribe to the basic concept that we are not in charge of the world, but God is, then we can stay sober." They suggested I needed to accept that my fear would leave when I was prepared to turn my will to a God of my understanding. It took me too many years to understand this and take the necessary risks without reservation. Until I did this, my willpower directed my dysfunctional life, which did not work out well.

Early in my recovery, it was challenging to maintain a new way of thinking and living. Although I had stopped consuming alcohol, my irrational fears and resentments would often surface unexpectedly. I wanted to be free of fear, but my dysfunctional instincts held me back. As I had always done for everything else, I relied on myself, never confident that God was interested in me or my problems.

Despite these struggles, I remained sober year after year. I realized that the recovery program was working for me and that I would be okay. I had survived much worse than this, and I would persevere. Eventually, I declared my willingness to do whatever was necessary to stay sober, including surrendering my will and life to God's care. I became humble and ready to ask God to remove all my shortcomings.

I had done all this—or so I thought—until one night at a recovery meeting, the speaker told the story of three frogs: Three frogs were sitting on a log floating in a pond. One of the frogs "made a decision" to jump into the pond. How many frogs remained on the log?

I started doing the math when I realized this was not a math problem but a philosophical one. Not one frog had jumped into the pond. One had only "made a decision." He was still sitting on the log! *That's me*, I thought. I had made the decision but had neglected to act. I had not turned over my fears, resentments, and character defects to my Higher Power. I had recited the words but did not act "as if" my problems were in his hands. I discovered I had to act and take the necessary steps to meet God halfway. I needed to bring my worry to God and have the faith to leave them there. I must think, act, and believe that my fears belong to God, who can handle them. This belief directly influenced my behavior. I use my imagination today and can see myself living without fear and apprehension. This beautiful feeling helps keep me sober. Today, my journey includes seeking the absence of fear and anxiety as I live my life while trusting and relying on a God of my understanding.

Receiving the gift of spirituality

As I continued to stay sober, I appreciated the benefits of maintaining a healthy spiritual life. The longer I remain sober, the better I feel and value my spirituality. My interior spiritual life required continuous work. I learned alcoholism is a three-fold disease affecting a person's physical, spiritual, and mental well-being. In my case, spirituality required the most attention because the damage was unseen and indescribable.

Many people in recovery report a profound and rapid shift in experiencing spirituality during their recovery. This was not the case with me. My progress was slow and steady, a day at a time. Nonetheless, I now recognize that spirituality is essential to those who stay sober and accept life on life's terms.

People in recovery who embraced spirituality appeared happy, kind, and loving and seemed to understand what I was going through. When suggestions about spirituality were presented, it was never more than what I could handle and just enough guidance to keep me coming back for more. Someone or something was looking out for me. All I had to do was show up and listen to learn.

Over the years, I have spoken with and read about many people in recovery, including priests, rabbis, philosophers, wise men, and women, to try and comprehend spirituality. I attended lectures, read countless books, and enrolled in meditation and theology classes, searching for spiritual direction. It was difficult for me to believe in a Higher Power or God when my starting point led me to an unhealthy, fearful, and unproductive way of responding to life's many challenges.

However, the recovery program taught me the value of a Higher Power and how I may imitate my Higher Power if I choose to do so. I was in no state of mind to develop a healthy lifestyle while I was blinded by alcohol and drugs. For many years, I tried and finally concluded that my approach was not working. I needed faith in a Higher Power to handle my problems. Like my control of alcohol, I could not do it alone and needed help.

That's a benefit of my recovery program, and I am doing my best to do the next right thing. It is painful to admit, but I had to drink every drink and use every drug to motivate me to seek the help I needed, join a recovery program, and hear the message of hope. I am grateful that I hit my emotional bottom when I did. I'm also thankful that I didn't take a life or cause permanent harm to anyone.

I have discovered that the image of God we create can either make or break us. I realize now that I had been searching for a relationship with a God of my understanding my entire life. One sign of God's presence is a desire for God. What was most reassuring for me to discover is that God had been with me for a long time, but I did not see him. I found that my perception of God was directly connected to and influenced how I viewed the world and relationships. My childhood conditioning resulted in a distorted, simplistic, punitive, exterior, and "out there" version of God.

During my recovery journey, I realized that I had been attempting to exert control not only over my father's behavior but also control over God. I had to acknowledge that not only was I trying to prevent my Dad's alcohol abuse, but I was dictating to God how I believed things should unfold in my father's life—demanding intervention according to my desires. This is not how God's will operates. As a result of this approach, I became frustrated and so angry that I cursed and turned away from God. I acknowledge that I was only a child, but this mindset has its consequences. I paid the price by feeling alone, without the presence of a higher power, living in an endless cycle of futile control followed by constant disappointment when I needed a refuge of hope.

My relationship with God has evolved into an interior experience. Before this, I lived in a world I had been trying to control with my will. I had to learn that I do not control what occurs in a constantly changing world. Prayer and meditation opened the door for me. Today, I focus on what I can control and let go of the rest.

I discovered this by associating with and learning from others in recovery. My Higher Power, God, speaks to me in words and emotions that are mine. I learned to rely on an inner authority with the values and compassion I have defined. An internal source whom I trust, who loves me unconditionally, and has a particular plan for my life. This is beautiful, freeing, and utterly different from that external "out there" punishing God I struggled with. My only job is to follow God's will for me each day.

With a clear and recovered mindset, I can establish a healthy connection that allows me to sense the presence of an internal God within me. The God I was confident had abandoned me is now present in my thoughts and emotions. I am aware of God's handiwork when I carry out God's will. I feel his presence when I witness or become a recipient of God's work through others. I have seen this many times in the past decades of sobriety, but I rarely recognized God's presence because I was blind to His grace. As a result of my sobriety, I can see things differently, which is another recovery gift. This gift was the one that the stranger on the beach urged me to accept. This is what I had been looking for—

an interior spiritual experience that results in happiness and the ability to thrive substance-free. Nothing material brings me the contentment and sobriety that I desire. My "higher power" remedied my dysfunctional thoughts and actions.

Once clueless, I transformed into someone who now has a moral compass that guides me. I shifted from having a hopeless condition of body and mind to being a person with principles and values that direct my thinking. I must try my best to fit into God's plan.

Without trying, the future takes care of itself, as I focus on today. The sun is going to rise and set without my input. God has a plan and a purpose for each of us. All I need to do is step out of the way and let it happen. I can wear the world, with its never-ending problems, like a loose garment, and it feels great.

When overwhelmed with fears, resentments, self-doubt, and negative thoughts, I have a simple formula conveyed to me by others in recovery. I pray and turn it over to my Higher Power and let go. I do not just decide, like the frog on the log—I do it! I struggle sometimes, but now I speak with another person in recovery to determine how to do the next right thing. I am no longer the traumatized kid or the rugged, independent guy who will fix everything himself. That lonely, futile, and unnecessary existence will lead me to alcohol. I know this because that is how I functioned for so long. Today, God is present within me, and I am grateful.

The Gift Goes On

I wish there were more straightforward ways to explain the most challenging part of my journey —my spirituality. At times, the tapes have played in my head, telling me I am not good enough and I should toss this memoir in the trash where it belongs. I have been at this long enough to know what I needed, so I prayed about this dilemma.

One evening, while writing, I received a text from a young man named Tim, whom I had met twelve years before. At that time, he and two of his college buddies were creating a film documentary for a class project on addiction. They interviewed me because I worked at a treatment program. Two of the guys were on time and prepared for the interview. One operated the camera while the other prepared questions for the interview. Tim was the third guy who arrived late, fumbled with the sound system and microphone, and was the least prepared of the three. Looking at him, I could see that he had not gotten much sleep the night before; he was the only one in the room sweating and had a mark on his face. I remember commenting, "Nice rug burn." He said he had been horsing around with friends the night before and did a face-plant in his living room. As he held the microphone and monitored the sound, I instinctively knew he had most likely been out drinking the night before. The rug burn mark on his face, his disheveled appearance, the smell of booze, and the "sweats" reminded me of someone I know all too well.

As the interview proceeded, I directed my message of alcoholism, recovery, and hope toward this kid. When the interview concluded, Tim asked several innocuous questions about alcoholism. After that, he left my office with the other two guys. I figured I would never see them again and wished them success on the project.

Shortly after the interview, I went to the parking area to leave for a lunchtime meeting. I was running late, hurrying to get to my appointment. Tim was still in the parking lot. He approached me and asked if he could ask a few additional questions. I nearly blew him off but reconsidered because I sensed he might have had enough of playing games with alcohol and was ready for a change.

Helping another alcoholic is vital to staying sober. Passing on the solution to another sick and suffering alcoholic offers the individual the opportunity to receive the gift of sobriety and helps keep them sober. The prayer of St. Francis reminds us that "it is in giving that we receive, and it is in pardoning that we are pardoned."

I canceled my lunchtime meeting because I saw this young man was hurting. We chatted, and I explained that I was in "recovery" and that my life had improved. I felt better about myself because I did not use alcohol. I told him I had those same rug burns, black eyes, and numerous cuts on my face and hands, but I had not experienced any embarrassing calamities since I stopped drinking. "My life is much better without alcohol." He was interested and asked me how I did it. I explained the format of the recovery group I attended and suggested he consider trying it. "Attend some meetings and call me in a week" to discuss his experience. We shook hands and parted ways, not knowing if I would ever hear from this kid again.

He attended the group and continued attending recovery meetings for the following year. I ran into him occasionally and offered words of encouragement. Then, he moved to the West Coast to start his career. That was a bold move, one that would have been too intimidating for me when I was his age. I would text him each year on his anniversary, hoping he was still sober and attending recovery meetings. I had no idea whether he was sober, so when I texted, I made assumptions and said the serenity prayer. Tim would reply to my text with gratitude that I remembered him on this special day. For the last twelve years, he has remained alcohol-free.

While writing this memoir and struggling to describe my spiritual journey, I received a text from Tim. It had been several years since we last talked. He enclosed a photo of his newborn baby boy. He said, "Was thinking about how if you didn't have the patience to talk to some raggedy kid twelve years ago in the parking lot on your way to your lunch break, this one might not be here." Then he added, "Thanks for being a good example of recovery that one day in September a while back."

That was it. This was the moment that it all came together for me. This is my Higher Power working through me to help another person. God's grace is present, and my inner spirituality is alive. Doing the next right thing brings me closer to my Higher Power. When accomplished anonymously, it is more meaningful for my inner spirituality and God. What a feeling of gratitude I had after reading Tim's text and seeing the picture of that child. This boy is fortunate because his dad is in recovery and has chosen not to drink. Tim has a loving family and is doing the next right thing for his wife and son by being sober. My Higher Power put me in the right place at the right time. That little boy has a better chance for a good life free from debilitating family trauma because his dad does not drink or abuse alcohol. I know that life is hard and, at times, not always on the level, but there's no reason this little boy's life cannot be different from that of that little boy from Logan Way.

This is where my living Higher Power thrives—my inner spirituality. This is where I made a connection to my Higher Power. No choirs of angels, burning bushes, or bright lights were glowing in the sky. Just an average recovering person from California sharing his gratitude because of a chat that started in a parking lot with another random sober guy twelve years before.

Once, in a meeting, someone said, "You may be the only version of a recovery program that a person will get to witness." It is also true that I may be the only version of a Higher Power that someone will see. I am not concerned if that person believes in my Higher Power. That is not the issue. The idea is to help other sick and suffering alcoholics gain freedom from alcoholism and drug dependency. We are all capable of doing our part. That is what happened with my friend Tim. (Is it a coincidence that this young man and I share the same first name? Who knows?)

When the people in the recovery program asked me to choose the values and qualities of a God of my understanding, I listed love, compassion, patience, kindness, tolerance, and forgiveness. Lots of sweet forgiveness because I needed it. The next question was to decide how that Higher Power works in my life. Is he out there or in here? The ability to choose the answer allows me to take things further and spread hope. Because I am in recovery, I can do this. I can live in the light. One of my program friends says it well, "Our spiritual experience has revolutionized our whole attitude toward life, other people, and God's universe. The essential thing in our lives is our certainty that God has entered our hearts and lives and is doing things in and through us that we could never do ourselves."

What progress have I made?

*"What progress, you ask, have I made? I have
begun to be a friend to myself."*
-Hecato of Rhodes, c. 100 BC

Writing about more than thirty years of recovery and sobriety
has been very challenging but has helped me grow. In my twenties,
I could never have imagined reaching the age of thirty. I celebrated
my thirtieth birthday by drinking for three days straight, grateful
that I was still alive despite my destructive behavior and what I
considered "bad luck." How can I best sum up thirty-plus years of
sobriety? It is not easy to summarize my life's ups and downs,
challenges, and opportunities I have experienced. However, I can
tell you that the past thirty-two years have been, without question,
the most beautiful years of my life.

Before achieving sobriety, I drank more, increasingly disliked
myself, and believed things would be different. But the battle I
fought was an internal struggle, not external events or
circumstances. I would lay out long-term, complex plans for the
next fight, but I craved alcohol, my magic potion. My recovery
sponsor compared it to stepping into a boxing ring, getting your
ass kicked, and returning to the ring, thinking the next fight would
be different. But when the next time came, the results were the
same. Instead of elaborate plans, all I had to do was not drink,
practice humility, be of service, focus on the present day, trust, and
rely on a High Power of my understanding.

When I was trying to determine whether alcohol was the
problem, my sponsor asked these questions: What happens when
you drink? Do you enjoy it? Deep down, I intuitively knew the

answers to those questions, and it became apparent that I had a drinking problem. Others also had the same responses to these questions, and I was not alone. My most significant action today is choosing not to drink alcohol or consume illicit substances. I have maintained my sobriety for over three decades, taking it one day at a time. I avoided that first drink because I knew it would destroy me.

Overcoming myself has been both my greatest challenge and my most significant accomplishment. I had to let go of alcohol and drugs and move forward with my life. Otherwise, alcohol would have destroyed me slowly and painfully. When I put down the drink, I began to appreciate the gift of life. These days, I regularly attend self-help meetings to strengthen my defense against that first drink. The sleeping beast inside me is alcoholism, and a single sip of alcohol will awaken the disease and demand more.

My internal self is now a safe harbor, not a violent storm of alcohol, drugs, and unhealthy emotions. Today, when I walk by my bedroom mirror, I smile as I remind myself it is just another day. I am just an average Joe, another Bozo on the bus, and I am perfectly content with that. The dark cloud no longer hangs over my head. What a contrast to the last night I drank, when I shamefully looked at myself in the mirror, spitting and shouting profanities, uttering those dreaded words, "I did it again." Today, those words are a thing of the past, and I have not had to repeat them for over thirty-two years.

I believe God brought me to a recovery program, and the people within that program brought me closer to God. I feel it every day, and I love it. The darkness of addiction and that bottomless, shameful pit of self-loathing has disappeared. Now, I enjoy living in the light of recovery and hope.

Now that I have gained all this insight into the consequences of growing up in a dysfunctional home and the origins of my behavior and attitude, I sometimes feel a mixture of sadness and anger. Who wouldn't? I often imagine alternative scenarios, wondering what life would be like if I did not possess the dysfunctional instincts and codependent traits common in those who grew up in alcoholic households. I have come to accept that I was once an active alcoholic, a people-pleasing workaholic, and a fear-driven individual whose choices were influenced by unhealthy and irrational decisions. Many, if not all, of the choices I made in my life, including decisions about education, careers, relationships, and even homeownership, were based on the survival skills I desperately grasped and learned as a child. Unfortunately, I carried these unhealthy reactionary decision-making patterns into adulthood. I was merely reacting to life, not actively shaping it. In some ways, I felt addicted to my brokenness because I could not move forward or find inner peace. This way of living did not protect me but contributed to my unhappiness and almost led to my downfall.

Fortunately, I learned a great deal during my journey of recovery. I now have the freedom to make choices based on my desires. I no longer must ask, "What flavor do you like?" when someone asks me what kind of ice cream I want. This is one glaring example of my people-pleasing codependent behavior that once had a hold on me. My attitude and outlook on life have shifted as I prioritize my happiness. I have realized that many individuals, even those considered "high functioning," continue to be controlled by the dysfunction and paralyzing fear from their past, allowing it to dictate their lives. How sad and unfulfilling my life would have been if I had held on to my childhood's dysfunctional rules and character traits.

What does my journey of recovery mean for me today? I am no longer enslaved by alcohol or drugs, and for that, I am grateful. I have adopted a manner of living that keeps me grounded with values and hopes inspired by my relationship with a God of my understanding. I am open to experiencing God's grace in my life. My fears, shame, and resentments are kept at bay because I have a Higher Power who loves me unconditionally and takes away my difficulties. The foundation for all of this is that I am enough. I do not need wealth, status, or power to validate myself. I am enough! I am no longer that alcoholic who loathes himself and utters those dreaded words, "I did it again." I've entirely accepted myself, and I am content with myself. Misguided instincts no longer drive me. Instead, I strive to be a compassionate and loving individual, a good friend to others. This transformation is a gift of humility. I can be there for others, and I'm grateful that others are there for me. I have invited them into my life. Life is a gift and no longer a burden.

Progress is hard to measure because it resides within me. I try to address my internal emotions in a healthy way and discuss them with my sponsor. I do not allow things to build up, which in the past resulted in me turning to alcohol to cope. I have been a work in progress for many years, and that is okay because I'm moving in the right direction, towards inner peace.

Everything changed when I accepted the message of recovery and the gift of a loving God. This newly discovered notion of God is central to me. Changing one's image of God has radically changed my sense of self and purpose. This journey is uniquely mine, and I am grateful for everything I have and don't have. The greatest gift is my healthy internal peace. I believe that it is the grace of God that has allowed me to experience this. I'm grateful to others who have taken the time and patience to listen to my call for help. Without them, I wouldn't be here today. Somehow, some way, all this keeps me sober.

It all comes together.

"If you are now wondering where to look for consolation, where to seek a new and better God...he does not come to us from books, he lives within us...This God is in you too. He is most particularly in you, the dejected and despairing."
Hermann Hesse

People in the recovery program provided the solution for my addiction. Fortunately, because of the gift of desperation, I stayed and listened. Despite sometimes clinging to my old ways, I decided to follow their path to sobriety.

The stranger on the beach encouraged me to "accept the gift." Still, I hesitated, clinging to my fears, doubts, insecurities, and stubborn resentments.

The revelation inspired by the story of the woman who touched the cloak of Jesus helped me realize that I wasn't damaged and that my Higher Power could heal me. That day, I overcame my shame and opened myself to a relationship with a Higher Power.

Listening to a man talk about forgiving his abusive mother and the gift he gave himself opened the door to my freedom. I let go of my anger, self-righteousness, and fear of disappointment and forgave my tormentor. My resentment towards my Dad vanished and was replaced with empathy and forgiveness.

The ability to help another alcoholic through service is another gift. I can help a young person whose alcoholic father is causing havoc by offering practical solutions and guidance on caring for themselves. When desperate parents reach out because their child is trapped in the ruthless world of substance abuse, I can offer helpful directions. Although this is not the road I would have chosen, it is mine, and with a positive attitude and a Higher Power, I will be all right. This keeps me sober and grateful.

When writing this memoir, I thought, what could God have done for me as a traumatized kid? What difference would that have made in my life? What if I could have experienced God as a loving and peaceful refuge instead of a punishing almighty being to battle and blame for all my problems? As a young man, I would have enjoyed knowing that love. Would having a Higher Power in my life change the circumstances and trajectory of my life?

I honestly believe the answer is yes. It would have changed my life and how I reacted to circumstances. Having a loving and compassionate God in my life would have helped. I would have had opportunities to learn, pursue exciting things, travel, explore nature, and engage in sports for enjoyment. (Not for neighborhood status or toxic masculinity.) I would have lived in the moment and not feared the future. I would have enjoyed my inner peace.

Thinking about this today, I can see several fundamental ways my life would have been different. I would have worried less and not been codependent, focusing on my needs rather than those of my alcoholic father. A child is not responsible for rescuing or saving their parents. Worrying never served me well and only robbed me of precious time to embrace the joys of childhood, which only happens once. I would have made healthy choices exploring things beyond my neighborhood rather than engaging in risky behaviors and thrill-seeking, such as hopping freight trains, burning abandoned cars, stealing, or participating in the dangerous games we played as kids.

Gaining some wisdom would have opened my eyes to the fact that I could not change the behavior or control an alcoholic or anyone else. Perhaps my Higher Power would have put a person in my life to model appropriate behavior, someone I could talk with to seek practical help to feel safe and react constructively. I would have acted differently with a positive role model.

Reflecting on this, I see that my Higher Power was working behind the scenes for me. Unfortunately, I tried everything possible to control the situation and interfere with God's work. I think about how often I tried to control my Dad's drinking and my own, expecting different outcomes, leading to disappointment and rage. I'll be honest: even to this day, I sometimes try to control people, places, and things. Thankfully, I recognized the futility and quickly let go, like dropping a red-hot frying pan. I leave the worrying to God.

Looking back at all my regrettable escapades, I believe God was working on my behalf; only I failed to see or acknowledge that possibility. This did not fit into my narrative of a punishing, transactional, and abandoning God. Admitting this takes humility and would be incompatible with my anger, disappointments, and resentment. Unhealthy emotions like these conceal God from me. To experience God's work and all the goodness in the world, I must live in the present, the here and now. I must change to experience God's miracles. Thankfully, I could alter my attitude, expectations, and inner disposition. Perhaps that's why the stranger on the beach urged me to "accept the gift." This gift opened the door to inner spirituality for him as it did for me. I also believe this gift of God is available to everyone, particularly those who have experienced failures, disappointments, humiliation, abuse, and trauma.

I'm convinced Jesus would support and actively participate in recovery meetings if he were on earth today. I picture Jesus helping alcoholics, drug addicts, prostitutes, sinners of all types, reprobates, and otherwise broken people, watching the remarkable transformation in their lives. There is Jesus, sitting among alcoholics, joking and laughing with people of different orientations, races, sizes, nationalities, the good, the evil, and the troubled, and offering his support. I imagine them gathered in a recovery meeting in some musty church basement, sharing their experiences of agony, defeat, despair, and, most importantly, hope. Jesus wants every alcoholic and traumatized person to be free from the chains of alcoholism and for every abused child to feel wanted and loved. One of the most agonizing feelings a person can experience is feeling unloved and unwanted.

In the Gospels, Jesus brings hope to sinners and the marginalized, outcasts, poor, and desperate alcoholics like me. This is where he witnesses the difficulties we experience in our everyday struggles and where his most powerful works occur. God wants all of us to recover and be liberated from our painful internal struggles and join him. He welcomed the outcasts, prostitutes, tax collectors, lepers, those without any spirituality, and those rejected by society because these were the individuals who needed him. Paraphrasing the Bible, those who are well do not need a doctor, but those who are sick do.

This is where miracles happen in the circumstances we encounter daily. It is in these situations that grace abounds. God is present in ordinary, simple settings. I believe he is also present in humiliating, lonely, and degrading places where alcoholics, including myself, have found themselves. The meaning of all of this is never to give up. A special reward and a solution to our problems are available if you are willing to accept a gift.

I have reached a pivotal point in my life where my previous distorted view of God has transformed into one of love, compassion, and support. Through my journey, I have grown and replaced my perception of a judgmental God with a loving one who created and accepted me just as I am. I now believe I am precisely what God intended when He made me.

I believe God's purpose for me may not align with what I had previously imagined. Suffering was not meant to be a part of His plan for me. My Higher Power guides me towards choosing love – the next right thing – and acting on His behalf when the opportunity arises.

The concept of God we hold in our hearts impacts every aspect of our lives. When I clung to a distorted version of God, it led me down a misguided path. This is how I viewed the world, resulting in distorted lived experiences. Recognizing this, I now understand how my previous toxic perception of God impacted my personality, self-esteem, and sense of purpose. This realization has brought positive changes. My perception of a benevolent God now serves as a guiding force in my life.

Today, when I envision God, I see Him embracing the young boy from Logan Way, and the grown man offering comfort with heartfelt words: "I'm sorry all of this happened to you." In this moment, there is no room for blame or shame--only understanding and compassion. It's the same for all alcoholics and their loved ones. He understands our pain and continues to provide unwavering support. His loving presence reassures me as he says, "Allow me to walk with you on this journey of recovery."

Epilogue

It's been over fifty years since I used that bright orange pith helmet to hitchhike rides to my lifeguard job in the summer of 1971. I was a confused and frightened seventeen-year-old kid starting his first real job with some responsibility and a paycheck. I was anxious to move into adulthood, autonomy, and freedom. Today, that lifeguard helmet is in perfect condition, sitting proudly on my bookcase at home. It brings a smile and symbolizes my independence, resilience, and success. It also reminds me of the nurturing care and compassion that I showed, as best I was able, to that frightened boy from Logan Way.

Who knows what would have happened that summer had I been assigned a job near my home and not at a beach twenty-four miles away? I would have had even more opportunities to drink and use drugs. I might have tossed that helmet away like everything I owned—just another meaningless item.

But today, that helmet means so much more because of the reasons I wanted that job and the risks I took to improve my situation. Perhaps it is a metaphor for my life. I played the cards I was dealt and made it to this day. As we say in recovery, I have a life second to none. I cannot say that my life is better or worse because of the entirety of my experiences, but it is mine, and I accept it. I have been tested by adversity and emerged on the other side. I am profoundly grateful for my life and everything that I have become. Considering the wisdom and spirituality I gained from sobriety, I am a grateful and wealthy man. I cannot put a price on my sobriety or inner peace. I love it when Susie H, a friend from my recovery group, gives a big hug while looking intently into my eyes and says, "Who has it better than us?" I can truthfully reply, "No one does." I have years of experience, a day at a time, free from alcohol, and I am so grateful for that. I was blind, but now I see.

I have often wondered why some children survive adverse childhood experiences while others do not. Why are some families irreparably torn apart and turned on each other? While others who experienced and shared the same trauma remain cordial and friendly? One of the many things I value is the loving relationship with my five brothers and their extended families. We get along well and communicate regularly with each other. Every six months, we gather for breakfast to check in and get updates on our families. There are also weekly phone calls and text messages between us.

Unfortunately, I know families with similar backgrounds and experiences who never speak to each other. In some families, the effects of someone else's alcoholism impact the next generation. I have also seen their adult lives destroyed because of the trauma they experienced as children, such as the two boys from my neighborhood that I described trying to get their dad home from a bar earlier. The younger brother developed an alcohol and drug problem. He was a "blackout drinker" who could never hold down a job and had a violent streak when drinking, just like his dad. He spent many years in state prison and now lives in a homeless shelter. Was his life over by age ten because of his traumatic experiences? The older brother, who had once been my friend, lived a quiet life, struggling to get by while raising his family in a trailer in another state. Unfortunately, his family lacked the resources to help him remain comfortable when he was dying of cancer.

When I think of these brothers and others from my neighborhood, I see what could have happened in my life. I know with certainty that that could easily have been me. I often wondered, why them and not me? I believe that through all my experiences, the one thing that made a difference for me was that I knew I was loved. Although I did not feel God's love, I did feel the love of other people present in my life. Unfortunately, for many, alcoholism can be more powerful than love, and like my Dad, they never get sober.

Even though our family has had problems with alcohol, as one of my older brothers likes to say, "The turkey doesn't go flying across the table on Thanksgiving Day." Several of my brothers attend recovery programs; two have long-term sobriety of forty-plus years. None of my brothers use alcohol, except one who drinks socially and can take it or leave it. We find it amusing when he leaves a half-empty glass of beer on the table, and we joke: "What is wrong with him? Was he adopted? Or did they accidentally take the wrong kid home from the maternity ward? Who the heck leaves beer in a glass? What a waste of good beer!" It's all good fun and a way to laugh at ourselves.

None of my brothers are divorced or have had to be forcibly removed from their homes by the police because of alcoholism. The police do not show up at their homes because of domestic abuse. They are all good parents and have loving and supportive relationships with their wives and children.

Getting together for family events is always an enjoyable time. I have five sisters-in-law and twenty-five nieces, nephews, and grandkids who have never seen their uncles intoxicated, humiliate themselves, or go into a drunken rage. With numerous birthdays, graduations, and holidays, many opportunities exist to show up for the people we love. We all look forward to getting together as a family. The love that we show one another is a benefit of sobriety. We never preach but live by example, which is remarkably successful. For the most part, none of the next generation knows the difficulties the Burke Boys experienced as children. (They will when they read this memoir, and I will sit with them and share the gratitude and forgiveness I have found.) Today, they witness our behavior and see how we broke the cycle of alcoholism in our family. My parents would be proud and grateful to see our loving family get-togethers.

I am fortunate to be in a loving relationship, something I have always desired. The decision of when, where, and with whom to be in this relationship was based on my authentic self rather than fear or dysfunctional thinking. I'm not entering a relationship to rescue another person. I love and am loved for who I am.

Moreover, all my material needs have been satisfied. Like most individuals, I grapple with my wants, but I am okay with that. I have accomplished everything I desired as a kid: a college education, advanced degrees, a successful career, cherished friends, healthy relationships, a beautiful home, and a comfortable retirement. I am a good friend to myself and treat myself with love and compassion. Sometimes, I am the loving parent I yearned for as a kid. I genuinely feel loved and accepted by my family and friends.

Most importantly, I have peace of mind and the ability to do the next right thing. I am grateful because, as we say in Boston, Sobah is Bettah! (Sober is better!) Perhaps God was looking out for me after all.

Had I not found the men and women in recovery, I could have ended up in jail, living a life of hopelessness, or perhaps dead. That is the end game for alcoholics imprisoned by their addiction. Alcoholism leads to a physically and emotionally lonely, painful death with no one to hold your hand, comfort you, or say "I Love you" as you pass from this world. That is what happened to Big John. He died alone without one final kiss of affection from his son. Alcoholism destroyed my relationship with him. "That stinking, lousy booze," as my Mom would say. Today, I understand he was a good man with a big problem. Alcoholism controlled him by separating this man from the love of his family. His painful and regrettable ending can never be undone but only forgiven. I forgive him, and I believe that he would have forgiven me.

I am blessed to have made it to this day and to share my story. I am grateful to continue my sobriety journey, one day at a time. I pray that your journey brings you sobriety, peace, and contentment.

"Don't drink. Go to a recovery meeting. Ask for help." –Anonymous.

THE END

Acknowledgments

I want to extend my heartfelt gratitude to two childhood friends from the Old Harbor Project whose authored works inspired me to pen down my own memoir-writing journey. Fran "Tiny" Fidler, the accomplished author of "Tiny's Wall," and Jake Manning, the creative mind of "Inside the Bricks," played a pivotal role in igniting my writing journey. Fran generously assisted by reading my memoir and providing invaluable editing insights. Additionally, I am indebted to my brother Brian, an aspiring writer, who consistently supported and encouraged me to persevere.

A special mention goes to Richard Rouse, a dear friend whose unwavering dedication was evident through his countless hours of reading and editing my work.

I am also grateful to all those who took the time to read my draft and provide candid feedback. Your contributions have been instrumental in shaping my memoir. I want to express my gratitude to my sponsors, Jack and Paul, two powers of example whose patience, generosity, and understanding helped to liberate me from the chains of alcoholism.

Lastly, a heartfelt thank you goes to Riky. Your support and encouragement have meant the world to me.

If you would like to contact me, my email is, OnLoganWay@gmail.com

Resources

Organizations that help people get sober and those affected by someone's drinking.

Alcoholics Anonymous: https://www.aa.org
Adult Children of Alcoholics: https://www.adultchildren.org
Al-Anon Family Group: https://www.al-anon.org/
SMART Recovery: https://www.smartrecovery.org/
Adverse Childhood Experiences (ACES) Study CDC:
https://www.cdc.gov/violenceprevention/aces/index.html

Photos

Below are pictures of Ladder 13 Boston Fire Department 1960-1980.

The ladder and tiller sections are the same. Only the cab was modernized and replaced.

(Photos courtesy of the Boston Fire Historical Society)

Engine 22 and Ladder 13.   Tremont Street, Boston, Ma.
(Photo courtesy of the Boston Fire Historical Society)

Dad's Boston Fire Department Helmet

My parents on their third wedding anniversary.

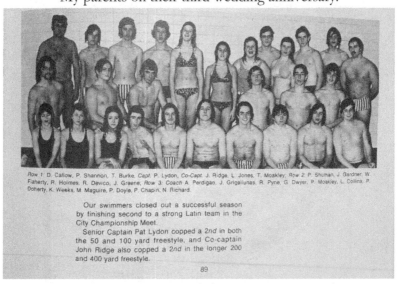

Row 1: D. Catlow, P. Shannon, T. Burke, Capt. P. Lydon, Co-Capt. J. Ridge, L. Jones, T. Moakley; Row 2: P. Shuman, J. Gardner, W. Flaherty, R. Holmes, R. Devico, J. Greene; Row 3: Coach A. Perdigao, J. Grigaliunas, R. Pyne, G. Dwyer, P. Moakley, L. Collins, P. Doherty, K. Weeks, M. Maguire, P. Doyle, P. Chapin, N. Richard.

Our swimmers closed out a successful season by finishing second to a strong Latin team in the City Championship Meet.

Senior Captain Pat Lydon copped a 2nd in both the 50 and 100 yard freestyle, and Co-captain John Ridge also copped a 2nd in the longer 200 and 400 yard freestyle.

89

South Boston High Swim Team 1972. That's me in the front row, six from the left

My initials are still on the door frame of our apartment in the Old Harbor project from 64 years ago. I was ten years old when I painted TB '64. This photo was taken in 2020.

My Life Guard helmet from 1971.

Mom with friends from the housing project. Top row 1st on the left.

Me at the Boys Club (front row, third from the right.)

Hanging out with my buddies in the project (Photo courtesy of Jake Manning)

Made in the USA
Las Vegas, NV
20 December 2023

83164842R00157